m

WILD BIRD GUIDES

Downy Woodpecker

WILD BIRD GUIDES

Downy Woodpecker

Gary Ritchison

STACKPOLE
BOOKS

For Tameria Dawn, Brandon Tyler,
and Brianna Carol

Published by
STACKPOLE BOOKS
5067 Ritter Road
Mechanicsburg, PA 17055
www.stackpolebooks.com

Printed in China

10 9 8 7 6 5 4 3 2 1

First edition

Illustrations by Erin O'Toole

Cover photo by Bill Marchel/Bill Marchel Outdoor Observations

Library of Congress Cataloging-in-Publication Data

Ritchison, Gary
    Downy Woodpecker / Gary Ritchison. — 1st ed.
      p.   cm. — (Wild bird guides)
    ISBN 0-8117-2724-6
    1. Downy woodpecker. I. Title. II. Series.
QL696.P56R58 1999   98-39595
598.7'2—dc21   CIP

Contents

Acknowledgments

Thanks to Jeff Hawkins, Carlo Abbruzzese, and Tom Mahan for working with me to learn more about Downy Woodpeckers. Financial support for this work was provided by the Kentucky Department of Fish and Wildlife Resources and the Department of Biological Sciences at Eastern Kentucky University. Thanks also to Jerred Seveyka for providing me with a copy of his poster, Rob Stark and Danielle Dodenhoff for sharing unpublished information and for reviewing chapter 4, Judy Ball for help with the literature search, and Dave Richwine and Mark Allison at Stackpole Books for all their efforts in putting together this series of Wild Bird Guides. Special thanks to my parents, Kenneth and Leona, for giving me a childhood close to nature and the love and financial support needed to pursue the career of my choice. Happy fiftieth wedding anniversary and good luck, Dad, with your continuing recovery. We're behind you 100 percent! Thanks also to Merrill Frydendall for being a terrific mentor; best wishes for a long and happy retirement. Finally, I thank my wife, Tameria Dawn, my son, Brandon Tyler, and my new daughter, Brianna Carol, for sharing my love of nature and for making our "nest" in Hilltop Acres a most delightful home.

1

An Introduction

"The principal characteristics of this little bird are diligence, familiarity, perseverance, and a strength and energy . . . which are truly astonishing. Mounted on the infected branch of an old apple tree, where insects have lodged their corroding and destructive brood in crevices between the bark and wood, he labours . . . incessantly at the same spot, before he has succeeded in dislodging and destroying them. . . . To a wren or a humming bird, the labour would be both toil and slavery, yet to him it is . . . pleasant and . . . amusing. The eagerness with which he traverses the upper and lower sides of the branches, the cheerfulness of his cry, and the liveliness of his motions while digging into the tree and dislodging the vermin, justify this belief." This is how the famous ornithologist Alexander Wilson described the Downy Woodpecker early in the nineteenth century. Other writers have also commented on the bird's diligence and strength. For example, John James Audubon noted that the downy was "not surpassed by any of its tribe in hardiness, industry, or vivacity."

The Downy Woodpecker is the smallest North American woodpecker and, in many parts of the United States and Canada, the most common one. Downies, more than most woodpeckers, use habitats altered and occupied by people, and as a result, they are our best-known and, for many, best-loved woodpecker. To paraphrase the words of Fannie Eckstorm, written in 1901, "no better little bird comes to our neighborhoods than our friend the Downy Woodpecker."

Downy Woodpeckers were formally described by the Swedish biologist Carolus Linnaeus in 1766 and given the scientific name *Picus pubescens.* The generic name *Picus* is Latin for "woodpecker." The name originated in ancient Roman mythology. Picus, the son of Saturn, was a prophet and god of the forest. An enchantress named Circe, daughter of Helios (the sun god) and Perse (a sea nymph), fell in love with Picus, but he rejected her. In revenge, Circe transformed Picus into a woodpecker.

The specific name *pubescens* is derived from the Latin *pubescena* and means "to become pubescent," or to put on the down of puberty. The term *down,* depending on the reference, refers either to the generally soft and downy appearance of this woodpecker's plumage or, specifically, to the soft feathers that cover the nostrils.

Since Linnaeus, the generic name of Downy Woodpeckers has been changed by ornithologists several times. For a while, downies were referred to as *Dryobates pubescens*, with the term *dryobates* derived from the Greek *drus* or *druos,* meaning "tree," and *bates* meaning "inhabitant." Later, downies went by the name *Dendrocopos pubescens. Dendrocopos* was derived from *dendron,* "tree," plus *kopos,* "striking or beating." Then, finally, in the 1983 checklist of North American birds published by the American Ornithologists' Union, the scientific name for downies became *Picoides pubescens. Picoides* means "resembling a woodpecker."

Adult Downy Woodpeckers are 5.5 to 6.5 inches (14 to 16.5 centimeters) long and weigh about 0.9 to 1.1 ounces (25 to 32 grams), with males and females similar in size. Downies are primarily black above but have a white stripe down the back and numerous white spots on the wings. The two central tail feathers are completely black. The remaining tail feathers have variable amounts of white, and the outermost tail feathers are largely white with some black barring. The throat and underparts are light, ranging from buffy white to grayish white, and have no markings. On the head, downies have white stripes both above and below the eyes.

Downy Woodpeckers are most often observed clinging to the side of a tree, and in that position, the pattern on their back is all that's visible. One function of that black and white pattern is to conceal downies from predators. The white stripe down the back sandwiched between the dark wings may represent a case of disruptive coloration. A sharp contrast in color patterns, like those on a downy's back, tends to reduce the contrast between a bird's shape or outline and its background. This may make it more difficult for a predator to recognize a downy on the side of a tree as a potential prey item.

The dappled pattern on the back may also allow downies to blend in with the background, or at least with some backgrounds. As one observer, Maurice Thompson, noted more than a hundred years ago: "I once saw a Goshawk pursuing a Downy Woodpecker, when the latter darted through a tuft of foliage and flattened itself close upon the body of a thick oak bough, where it remained as motionless as the bark itself. The hawk alighted on the same bough within two feet of its intended victim, and remained sitting there for some minutes, evidently looking in vain for it, with nothing but thin air between monster and morsel. The woodpecker was stretched longitudinally on the bough, its tail and beak close to the bark, its black and white speckled feathers looking like a continuation of the wrinkles and lichen."

The pattern on the back of a downy's head also serves another function. Each bird has a unique pattern, and it is likely that downies use them to recognize particular individuals. The ability to recognize individuals is common among birds and can be very useful. For example, such recognition allows a Downy Woodpecker to quickly tell whether another downy observed in its territory, or perhaps near a nest or roost cavity, is a friend—perhaps a mate—or a foe such as an intruding downy possibly looking for a place to establish its own territory. A downy unable to recognize other individuals would often respond inappropriately in such situations. Because recognition of other individuals is so important, downies do not depend entirely on visual cues. Other cues, such as individually distinct vocalizations, are also used.

Male and female downies are similar in appearance, but females have slightly longer tails, and males have a red patch on the back of the head or nape. Longer tails may permit female downies to save a little energy. Females usually spend more time on the vertical surfaces of tree trunks and large limbs than do males, and on such surfaces the tail serves as a brace. A longer tail, or brace, lessens the tendency of gravity to pull a woodpecker out away from the vertical surface, which means a female expends less energy maintaining her hold on the trunk or branch.

The plumage of juvenile downies at fledging is similar to that of adults, although the black areas are duller and browner, the underparts more grayish or buffy, and the sides of the breast and the flanks finely streaked. Young males also have reddish or pinkish feather tips on the crown, but not on the back of the head like adult males. Young females have brownish black crowns, either unmarked or with white or buffy spots. Young downies also differ from adults in eye color; juveniles have a pale or olive-brown iris, and adults usually have a brown or brown-red iris. Young downies typically undergo molt during late summer and early fall and lose their juvenile appearance. By October, most juveniles have completed molt and resemble adults.

Species in which males and females differ in coloration are called sexually dichromatic. In contrast to many dichromatic species of birds, the difference between male and female Downy Woodpeckers is modest; males have a patch of red on the back of the head and females do not. Many other woodpeckers also exhibit rather limited differences in the appearance of males and females. Experiments have revealed, however, that these apparently slight differences are clearly recognized by the woodpeckers. For example, the only difference between male and female Northern Flickers is a small black or red streak or "mustache" on the side of the male's head. To determine whether flickers use this mark for sex recognition, an investigator captured a female and, using black paint, added a mustache. When released, the mate of this unlucky female attacked her as though she were an intruding male. In the same manner, Downy Woodpeckers use the presence or absence of the red patch to determine the sex of other downies.

In contrast to most sexually dichromatic species of birds, the "badge" that advertises a Downy Woodpecker's sex does not appear to be very conspicuous. In fact, when two downies face each other for the first time, they may not be able to determine the other individual's sex because their badge is on the back of the head. Often, however, downies are likely to discern the sex of an approaching individual through vocalizations. And if approaching downies happen to land in adjacent or nearby trees, the back of the other bird would actually be easier to see than the front. In addition, male downies can make their badges more obvious from the front by elevating the colored feathers in a crest-raising display. So a back-of-the-head badge may not, under some circumstances, be all that inconspicuous.

Under other circumstances, it may be beneficial to keep the badge as inconspicuous as possible, by facing another downy in such a way that the badge is not visible or, at least, only partially visible, or depressing the colored feathers as much as possible (the opposite of the crest-raising display). Male downies can do this, so the red patch can be classified as a "coverable badge." Other species of birds also have such badges. Eastern Kingbirds and male Ruby-crowned Kinglets have crown patches that, by repositioning adjacent feathers, can either be exposed or concealed. The advantage of a coverable badge is that in addition to advertising sex, the badge may signal aggression, and sometimes it's better not to do so. A young male Downy Woodpecker that disperses from his parents' territory in search of his own may inadvertently pass through the territories of other adult males. If detected by these resident males, a young male can signal submissiveness by covering his badge and, by so doing, avoid a potentially costly interaction in terms of both energy and possible injury. During any circumstance when it would be better to avoid conflict, a male Downy Woodpecker can cover his badge.

Male Downy Woodpeckers get the red coloration for their patches from pigments called carotenoids. Surprisingly, birds cannot synthesize carotenoid pigments and must obtain them from their foods, particularly ones that are orange or red. Ingested carotenoids are then deposited in feathers during molt when new feathers are developing, and studies of other species have revealed that the amount of carotenoids ingested influences plumage coloration. In the case of birds with red coloration, ingesting more carotenoids produces brighter reds.

If this is also the case in Downy Woodpeckers, the quality of a male's red patch could be linked to his diet. This would be significant, because the quality of a bird's diet reflects several important characteristics, including competitive ability, foraging skills, coordination, vision, and disease resistance. A higher-quality individual is likely to have a better-quality diet and therefore better-quality plumage. Thus a large, especially bright red patch may indicate a particularly high-quality male downy. If so, the male downy's badge may provide information to other downies about a male's relative quality. Such information could play an important role in female mate choice, with females choosing mates based on the relative quality of their patches, and in male-male interactions, with males having higher-quality patches tending to be dominant over those with lower-quality patches.

When pecking wood, a downy draws its head back, then shoots it forward, perhaps at speeds approaching 20 feet per second or more, until the bill strikes the substrate. This impact, depending on the consistency of the wood, may result in a very rapid deceleration of the head. Yet, amazingly, downies suffer neither brain damage nor headaches.

Some woodpeckers, such as Acorn Woodpeckers, appear to peck in a straight line, with the bill coming straight into the substrate. This pecking trajectory, once thought to be common among woodpeckers, may be potentially less damaging, because it would protect the brain from harmful rotational forces. Nevertheless, though potentially more damaging, pecking in an arc is more effective, in terms of generating momentum and greater force, than pecking in a straight line. To illustrate this, imagine trying to drive a nail into a piece of wood. Which would be easier: moving a hammer straight back from the nail, then forward into the nail, or moving the hammer back in an arc, then swinging it forward into the nail? Obviously, moving the hammer through an arc is more effective. In the same manner, woodpeckers can peck more effectively by moving their heads through an arc.

Recent work by Jerred Seveyka at the University of Montana indicates that many woodpeckers, including downies, move their heads through an arc when pecking. Doing so increases the rotational forces acting on the woodpecker brain and would seem to increase the risk of brain injury. Damage from rotational acceleration can occur when the skull suddenly rotates. Because the brain, like all objects with mass, has inertia, it tends to remain stationary inside the skull. This can cause a shearing effect where the brain is attached to the skull, potentially causing damage. Nevertheless, woodpeckers do not suffer such damage.

The woodpecker brain is protected in several ways from the forces generated by repeated pecking. First, as noted by Hans Winkler and colleagues, the woodpecker brain is proportionately small, at least compared with the human brain, and as a result, the mass-to-surface-area ratio is low (there is a lot of surface area relative to the brain's weight). This means that any impact forces, such as when the brain strikes the inner walls of the skull, are distributed over a relatively greater area, making the woodpecker brain perhaps fifty to one hundred times less vulnerable to impact injuries than the human brain. The relatively small size of the woodpecker brain also limits rotational forces.

Woodpeckers also have little cerebrospinal fluid. This fluid is located in small cavities in the brain, called ventricles, and in the area between the brain and the skull. This fluid is more plentiful in mammals and serves to cushion the mammalian brain; however, the presence of this fluid can cause problems when a mammal receives a hard blow to the head, such as when a boxer is hit on the forehead. The fluid does provide protection on the struck side of the brain. On the opposite side, however, the sudden backward movement of the skull causes it to momentarily pull away from the brain, creating a temporary vacuum. Then, when the skull is no longer moving in response to the blow, the vacuum suddenly collapses, and the brain rebounds back and may strike the inner surface of the skull with sufficient force to cause damage. This phenomenon is called contrecoup and explains why damage to boxers' brains often occurs at the back of the brain rather than the front.

Because woodpeckers have little cerebrospinal fluid, there is relatively less movement of the brain relative to the skull. As a result, when a woodpecker strikes a substrate with its bill, no vacuum develops between the skull and the back of the brain and there is little likelihood of injury to that area of the brain.

The structure and musculature of the skull also protect the woodpecker's brain. When woodpeckers strike a substrate, small muscles at the back of the lower jaw, or mandible, plus the arrangement of bones in the woodpecker skull tend to transmit the impact forces below the brain to the base and back of the skull. These areas of the woodpecker skull are relatively thick and dense and probably transmit these forces to the neck and not to the brain.

The lifestyle of Downy Woodpeckers is reflected in other areas besides the head and bill. Downies and other woodpeckers have thicker skin than most birds, necessary because most woodpeckers are frequently in contact with the rough bark of trees. In addition, downies sometimes feed on ants, many of which can deliver potentially painful bites.

The woodpecker tail is modified for climbing and clinging. The tail bone, called the pygostyle, and vertebrae in the tail are relatively large, as are the muscles that attach to them. These large muscles are needed because the tail serves as a prop, supporting the weight of the woodpecker against vertical, or nearly vertical, surfaces. To enhance the tail's function as a prop, the tail feathers that insert on the pygostyle, especially the middle ones, are very stiff. Those middle feathers also have pointed tips and are curved slightly inward, ensuring that the tail makes solid contact with the substrate.

Downy Woodpeckers have other characteristics that serve them well as they extract prey from the nooks and crannies of trees and other substrates, including zygodactyl feet (two toes in front and two behind), chisel-like bills, and very long tongues with spearlike tips. Like other living organisms, Downy Woodpeckers are products of a long evolutionary process, and each downy does its best to survive and reproduce. The ways in which Downy Woodpeckers do this are often intriguing and always interesting.

2

Taxonomy and Distribution

Species of birds like Downy Woodpeckers that have broad geographic distributions are commonly divided into sub-species because groups of individuals separated for some time from other such groups often develop different characteristics. Recent studies suggest, however, that there is little genetic variation among the seven subspecies of Downy Woodpeckers. One possible explanation for this genetic similarity is that a relatively small population of downies rapidly colonized much of North America. It is also possible, although perhaps less likely, that a recent favorable mutation rapidly swept through the species range and eliminated any preexisting genetic variation.

The genus *Picoides* includes more than thirty species of woodpeckers distributed through-out the world. Nine of these species, including Downy Woodpeckers (*P. pubescens*), can be found in North America. The other eight species include Hairy Woodpeckers (*P. villosus*), Ladder-backed Woodpeckers (*P. scalaris*), Nuttall's Woodpeckers (*P. nuttallii*), Strickland's Wood-peckers (*P. stricklandi*), Red-cockaded Woodpeckers (*P. borealis*), White-headed Woodpeckers (*P. albolarvatus*), Three-toed Woodpeckers (*P. tridactylus*), and Black-backed Woodpeckers (*P. arcticus*).

Hairy Woodpeckers (left) can be found throughout the range of Downy Woodpeckers, and these two species exhibit strikingly similar plumage. Hairy Wood-peckers are larger than downies, but this difference may not be apparent unless the two species are observed together. More helpful in distinguishing these two woodpeckers is the difference in bill proportions. The downy's bill is very short, and the head is at least twice as long (front to back) as the bill. The hairy's bill is much longer—nearly as long as the head—and more chisel-like.

The calls of these two species are also similar but differ in quality. Both species utter brief contact notes. For downies, this call sounds like *pick;* the hairy version is a bit sharper and sounds like *peek.* Each species also has a rattle or whinny call. The downy's version of this call consists of a rapid series of notes that gradually descend in pitch; the notes in a hairy's rattle stay more or less at the same pitch.

The other seven species of North American woodpeckers in the genus *Picoides* bear less resemblance to downies and have more restricted ranges than downies or hairies. Whereas both downies and hairies have a vertical white stripe down the back, the other species have either completely dark backs or ladder backs, with a series of horizontal, alternately light and dark streaks. The ranges of three species, the Ladder-backed (top left), Nuttall's (top right), and Strickland's Woodpeckers, are limited to parts of the southwestern United States and Mexico. White-headed Woodpeckers (bottom left) are limited to coniferous forests of California, Oregon, and Washington.

Black-backed (top left) and Three-toed Woodpeckers (top right) are found primarily in the coniferous forests of Canada and the western United States. The Red-cockaded Woodpecker (bottom) is an endangered species of the southeastern U.S. This species was once common but has declined drastically in numbers and distribution because many of the mature, open pine forests on which this species depends have been cut for timber.

Downy Woodpeckers also bear some resemblance to other common, but less closely related, species of woodpeckers. Red-bellied Woodpeckers (left) are found throughout the eastern United States and are especially common in the Southeast. The red-belly is larger than the downy and has a reddish orange cap and a ladder back. Red-headed Woodpeckers inhabit open deciduous forests in the eastern United States. These birds are also larger than downies and have bright red heads. Northern Flickers are typically found in more open habitats than downies and are much larger. The flicker has a brown back with horizontal black streaks, a spotted breast and abdomen, and a white rump. The Yellow-bellied Sapsucker (right) is just slightly larger than the downy but has a ladder back and a narrow vertical white stripe on the wing (not on the back).

Groups of related genera are placed in common subfamilies and families, with Downy Woodpeckers placed in the family Picidae and the subfamily Picinae. This subfamily includes several genera of woodpeckers, including *Melanerpes* (Red-bellied, Golden-fronted, and Gila Woodpeckers), *Sphyrapicus* (sapsuckers), *Colaptes* (flickers), *Dryocopus* (Pileated Woodpecker), and, of course, *Picoides*. Families include a number of related subfamilies and the Downy Woodpecker family, Picidae, includes the woodpeckers, wrynecks, and piculets. Piculets, all tropical species, are tiny woodpeckers with short tails that are not used as props. Wrynecks, so named because of their rather flexible necks, are less woodpecker-like, with short, slightly curved bills. There are only two species of wrynecks, one that breeds throughout much of northern Europe and Asia and the other in Africa. Picids, along with many other families (including the Toucan family, Ramphastidae), are also members of the order Piciformes.

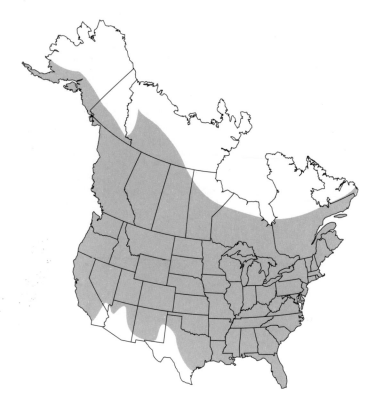

Downy Woodpeckers can be found throughout much of the United States and Canada but are most common in the eastern United States. Downies are not found in the drier habitats of the Southwest or West or in northern Alaska or Hawaii. In Canada, the northern limit of their range extends west from southern Yukon across northern Alberta and Saskatchewan, central Manitoba, northern Ontario, and southern Quebec to Newfoundland. Downies are most abundant in the humid regions of the eastern United States where the average January temperature is warmer than –10 degrees F (–21 degrees C). Numbers also decline as vegetation changes from forest to grasslands, tundra, or desert.

Because they forage primarily by gleaning from bark and excavating, the ability of downies to obtain food is less affected by deep snow and cold temperatures than it is for ground foragers. Thus, the northern range limit of downies, unlike those of other species, such as Northern Cardinals, has not been influenced by winter feeding by humans. On a local scale, however, winter feeding may increase densities of Downy Woodpeckers by attracting individuals from surrounding areas and by improving survival rates.

Winter can be a difficult time for small birds at northern latitudes because they must maintain high metabolic rates and high rates of energy consumption at a time when there may be less food and fewer hours of daylight to forage. In addition, small birds tend to lose heat more rapidly than larger birds because small birds have more surface area per unit weight. As a result, Downy Woodpeckers increase in size with increasing latitude, downies in Alaska being about 12 percent larger than downies in Florida. Survival under such conditions still requires physiological adjustments. One possible strategy would be to store more fat during the winter, to provide more insulation and energy during particularly harsh weather.

Downy Woodpeckers, unlike some species of birds, do not appear to increase stores of fat during cold periods, however. In general, ground-foraging birds are more likely to increase fat stores during the winter than are tree-foraging birds like woodpeckers, perhaps because snowfall is less likely to affect access to food in trees than to food on the ground. Despite the absence of extra fat, downies are better able to maintain their body temperature and thus are more tolerant of cold during the winter. This increased tolerance is likely due to an increased ability to generate heat, and downies may do this by increasing their muscle mass during the winter. This muscle, in turn, can generate additional heat via shivering.

A bird's habitat consists of a complex array of living, or biotic, and nonliving, or abiotic, factors. Among the nonliving factors are temperature and precipitation; living factors include things like the quantity and quality of various types of food and the type and numbers of predators. Some species of woodpeckers have very specific habitat requirements. For example, Red-cockaded Woodpeckers typically require open, parklike pine forests at least 80 to 120 years old. In addition, these woodpeckers almost always nest and roost in cavities excavated in living, mature pines whose heartwood has been destroyed by a fungus.

Other species, like Downy Woodpeckers, have much broader habitat requirements. Downies can be found in a wide range of habitats, ranging from cities to deciduous forests to cypress swamps to pine plantations. Despite this tolerance for a variety of habitats, however, downies do exhibit preferences. Downy Woodpeckers in Oregon are found primarily in deciduous stands of aspen or in cottonwoods along streams and rivers. In Maryland, the habitat of downies is described as wood margins, open woodland, and forest edge. In Tennessee, downies select forests with abundant understory vegetation. Downy Woodpeckers in Virginia also prefer younger forests with a lot of understory.

Because downies nest in cavities constructed in either totally or partially dead small trees, their territory must have some snags—trees where many of the branches have fallen off or are present but no longer have foliage. Appropriate snags for downies are about 6 to 12 inches in diameter and 6 to 60 feet high. Because downies may use several snags per year for nesting and roosting, and also like to forage on snags, good Downy Woodpecker habitat should have at least four or five snags per acre.

Downy Woodpecker habitat must also contain suitable foraging sites. Downies are very much foraging generalists and can use a variety of tree species. Downies can also forage on limbs of just about any diameter and at almost any height, although they often prefer to feed lower in trees. Thus many forested areas provide adequate foraging habitat for downies.

Downy Woodpeckers do occur in urban areas. Although numbers vary with factors such as the age of an urban area, which would generally be correlated with the number and size of trees and other vegetation in an area, downies are typically not as abundant in urban areas as in more natural areas. Most urban areas are dominated by grass lawns and have relatively low densities of trees and shrubs. Such areas provide little foraging habitat for downies. In addition, urban areas often have many non-native trees, often fruit trees, and these provide less food for downies because such trees support fewer insect species than native trees. Also missing from urban areas are snags, as dead or dying trees are quickly removed by most homeowners. Without snags, downies have few or no places to nest, and fewer areas to forage. Thus, though urban areas located near natural areas may be visited by downies, such as when obtaining seeds or suet at feeding stations, these woodpeckers often spend much of their time—and nest—in the natural area and not the urban area.

3

Food and Feeding Habits

Birds have high metabolic rates and use energy at high rates. As a result, they must eat frequently and select and digest food efficiently. Downy Woodpeckers are no exception, and they exhibit several adaptations that enhance their foraging efficiency, among the most obvious of which is the bill.

The skull and bill of downies represent an intricate compromise between weight and strength. They contain numerous air spaces (spongy bone) that minimize weight, and weight reduction has undoubtedly been an important factor in the evolution of avian flight. The bill also contains numerous bony struts, called trabeculae, that reinforce it and enable it to withstand the substantial forces that may result when downies pound against a tree.

In woodpeckers that regularly drill and excavate, such as downies, these trabeculae are particularly numerous, longitudinally oriented, and strongly calcified near the tip of the bill. In addition, the bill of the Downy Woodpecker is straight and tapers to a chisel-like tip that permits efficient excavation. And the arrangement of the cells growing at the end of the bill is such that the cutting edges at the bill tip are self-sharpening.

As downies drill or excavate, small pieces of wood may fly out in all directions. To prevent these pieces from entering the nostrils, located at the base of the bill, downies and other woodpeckers have tufts of feathers over both nostrils. To help protect the eyes, downies have a third eyelid, called the nictitans, visible in this photo. This membrane provides protection by completely or partially covering the eye, as well as by gently brushing the surface of the eye with tears to remove any particles.

Once a foraging downy exposes the tunnels of wood-boring larvae, it uses its specialized tongue to extract the larvae. The tongue of the Downy Woodpecker is slender, rounded, and flexible and can be extended well beyond the tip of the bill. This is possible because the tongue is attached to an extremely long complex of bones known as a hyoid. The hyoid has two horns, or forks, that extend backward from the base of the tongue and curve around the back of the skull, pass over the top of the skull, and coil around the eye as shown above. Posteriorly, the tongue is enclosed in a muscular sheath, and this muscle is used to extend the tongue.

The tip of the downy's tongue is very sensitive to touch and also possesses backward-directed barbs. As a result, the downy can use its tongue to both detect and capture larvae. Once detected, larvae impaled by the tip of the tongue are held firmly and are unlikely to escape as the tongue is withdrawn back into the mouth. During protrusion, the tongue is also coated with a sticky mucus secreted by large salivary glands, further enhancing a downy's chance of successfully capturing small insects.

After a Downy Woodpecker swallows an insect or other food item, it passes through a muscular tube called the esophagus and into the stomach. A bird's stomach has two parts: an anterior portion with a lining that secretes digestive juices and a posterior portion with muscular walls. The anterior portion, called the proventriculus, is particularly well developed in birds that eat lots of insects, like the Downy Woodpecker. The proventriculus secretes acids and enzymes that are particularly effective at digesting proteins, a primary constituent of insects. The posterior portion, or gizzard, serves as the avian equivalent of teeth and is used to grind and digest hard food items. Although present in downies, gizzards are generally better developed in seed-eating birds. Once food enters the gizzard, the muscular walls contract and relax, churning and grinding the contents. To enhance the grinding action, the gizzard has a hard, rough inner surface.

After it is pulverized in the gizzard, food passes into the intestine. Downy Woodpeckers and other largely insectivorous birds typically have shorter intestines than those that feed primarily on seeds. This is because protein-rich foods, such as insects, are partially digested by enzymes in the proventriculus. Less time is needed, therefore, to complete digestion in the intestine. Once digested, food is absorbed through the walls of the intestine and distributed in the blood to the rest of the body.

Although their bills and digestive systems are specialized for feeding on insects, Downy Woodpeckers feed on a wide variety of plants and animals. In 1911, researcher Foster Beal examined the contents of 723 Downy Woodpecker stomachs, collected over an entire year, and found that their diet consisted of about 76 percent animal matter and 24 percent vegetable matter. The animal matter consisted predominantly of insects, including beetles (both adults and larvae), weevils, ants, scale insects or bark lice, aphids, and butterfly and moth larvae. Downies also consumed the eggs of grasshoppers, crickets, katydids, and cockroaches. Overall, downies fed on at least forty-four different kinds of insects. Other animal matter included spiders, millipedes, sow bugs, and a few snails.

Downy Woodpeckers also fed on twenty different kinds of plants. This vegetable matter consisted primarily of seeds, including acorns, beechnuts, hazelnuts, corn, and sunflower seeds, and wild fruits, including blackberries, elderberries, blueberries, and those of poison ivy, poison oak, flowering dogwood, and rough-leaved dogwood. More recent studies have provided similar results. In one study, adult beetles (Coleopterans) and ants were the most frequently eaten insects and corn the most frequently eaten plant material.

Downies also feed on animal fat from carcasses when it is available.

Downy Woodpeckers use several different foraging techniques to obtain food. One common technique is called peer and poke, or gleaning, and does not require penetration of bark. When foraging in this manner, downies carefully examine the substrate, including cracks and crevices, and pick off any prey items they detect, such as small insects or insect eggs. Another technique is pecking, or tapping, which involves driving the bill against the substrate but not penetrating very deeply. Downies may use the reverberation caused by pecking to detect underlying tunnels created by wood-boring insects. Pecking may also cause the prey to move, making it easier for downies to locate. Yet another technique used by Downy Woodpeckers is scaling, in which downies search for prey items by using their bills to remove small pieces of bark. Downies also excavate, or dig beneath the surface of the bark or other substrate, in search of prey. Downies are sometimes observed excavating into goldenrod ball galls (bottom right). Certain insects cause plants to form these galls,

within which the larvae of these insects subsequently feed, grow, and develop. Downies tunnel into these galls to extract the larvae within the central cavity. Infrequently, downies hawk, or sally, which involves flying from a perch to capture flying insects.

Foraging Downy Woodpeckers often climb up to or near the top of one tree, then fly down toward the bottom of the next tree. This pattern of movement is no doubt favored because it takes less energy than does climbing down a tree and flying up toward the top of the next tree. Part of the potential energy gained by the downy in climbing upward against the force of gravity can subsequently be used in moving to the next tree. Downies flying down take advantage of gravity, which means less expenditure of energy.

With their stiff tail feathers and relatively short legs, downies and other woodpeckers are better adapted for climbing up trees than down. A woodpecker attempting to climb down a tree would have problems with its tail catching on rough bark. If a downy tried to back down a tree, it would not be able to see where to grasp the bark with its feet and it would scare off much of its potential prey before getting into a position where it could capture them.

Downies forage primarily on trees but occasionally forage on shrubs and a variety of other plants, including mullein, cornstalks, and goldenrod. Many species of trees are used by foraging downies, with different tree species used in different parts of their range. Downies often forage on smaller branches and twigs but also forage on larger branches and trunks. Foraging height can range from near the ground to the tops of very large trees. Downies are very agile foragers, sometimes even hanging upside down. Foraging downies often focus their attention on crooked and leaning trees, broken stubs, and discolored surfaces, perhaps because such areas are more likely to be infested with insects.

Several studies have revealed differences in the foraging behavior of male and female Downy Woodpeckers. In one study in central Illinois, males foraged on a greater variety of trees and usually pecked for food on small limbs, whereas females used the peer and poke technique, probing bark crevices of trunks and larger branches. In a Kansas study, males tended to forage on smaller branches, usually less than 2 inches in diameter, and females foraged on trunks and larger limbs.

Rather than being genetically determined, the differences in the foraging behavior of male and female Downy Woodpeckers appear to be the result of male dominance: Males use the smaller limbs typically preferred by downies and force females to use the larger limbs and trunks of trees. Studies have demonstrated that female Downy Wood-peckers forage much like males when males are absent. Studies in which males and females were observed foraging in both the presence and absence of the other sex showed that although male foraging behavior was not affected by the presence of females, females foraged on smaller limbs when males were absent. Male Downy Woodpeckers also have been observed supplanting females, flying to a female's position and forcing her to move, indicating that males are indeed dominant over females.

Although differences in foraging behavior and prey use help reduce competition between male and female Downy Woodpeckers, males obviously benefit more than females because they have access to the preferred foraging sites. As a result, males may be in better condition than females, particularly during the winter. Females, therefore, must attempt to minimize the potential adverse effects of being excluded from those preferred sites, particularly when food is most scarce, as in midwinter. One obvious strategy used by female Downy Woodpeckers is to try to avoid males during such periods so that they can forage in the more preferred sites.

The presence of other, larger species of woodpeckers may influence the foraging behavior of both male and female Downy Woodpeckers. A study in Illinois revealed that downies foraged lower in trees and were more likely to forage on smaller understory trees when Red-headed Woodpeckers were present. During periods of food scarcity, Downy Woodpeckers may try to avoid larger species so that they can forage on the smaller limbs higher in the canopy that they generally prefer.

The foraging behavior of Downy Woodpeckers changes throughout the year. During the winter, downies may use the pecking and excavating techniques, which allow them to penetrate trees deeper than either the peer and poke or the scaling method, more frequently than during the warmer months. Greater penetration is needed during the winter because fewer prey are available on the surface of the bark.

Downies may also forage more on trees with rough bark during the winter. Rough bark provides invertebrates with more protection from cold temperatures than does smooth bark, so rough-barked trees likely contain more prey. Downies may also forage more on dead trees during the winter, perhaps because many invertebrates overwinter within these trees. In general, as temperature decreases and wind velocity increases, downies make fewer foraging movements and spend more time at each location. This may be an attempt to remain in more protected locations to avoid harsh conditions, but it is also possible that downies are moving less because they are foraging on substrates that take longer to search.

During the winter, Downy Woodpeckers may forage alone, with their mates, or with mixed-species flocks. Although species composition varies with location, these flocks may include Black-capped or Carolina Chickadees, Tufted Titmice, White-breasted Nuthatches, Golden- and Ruby-crowned Kinglets, Brown Creepers, Hairy Woodpeckers, and Downy Woodpeckers. These groups of largely insect-eating birds are loosely organized, and flock composition varies during the day as individuals temporarily join then leave as the flock moves through the ranges or territories of different birds. Chickadees and titmice are commonly referred to as the nuclear species because they typically form the basic nucleus of these flocks, and their presence attracts follower species like Downy Woodpeckers. Individuals in these flocks generally remain several feet or more apart. Flocks move rather slowly through woods, often covering about 300 to 1,500 feet in an hour.

Downy Woodpeckers in winter flocks capture prey at higher rates than when they forage alone. Foraging success increases because downies spend more time foraging and less time looking for potential predators when in a flock, and other flock members enjoy the same benefit. Each individual in a flock can be less vigilant because the other flock members help watch for predators. Collectively, the vigilance level of the flock remains high, and approaching predators are more likely to be detected by flocks than by solitary individuals.

Despite the advantages of foraging in a flock, Downy Woodpeckers sometimes forage alone. Downies maintain and defend territories throughout the year. A downy may join a flock when it passes through its territory but drops out when the flock moves out of the territory and into the territory of another downy.

In contrast to several other species of woodpeckers, Downy Woodpeckers rarely store or cache food items. Storing and later retrieving food items requires a good memory, and an area of the brain known to be important in memory, the hippocampal complex, or dorsomedial cortex, is typically well developed in birds, such as Red-bellied Woodpeckers, that regularly store food. The hippocampal complex of the non-food-storing Downy Woodpecker is also relatively large, possibly because downies engage in other activities that require a good memory. Downies may benefit from remembering when they last fed at a particular site because, given sufficient time, insect populations can become reestablished. Although it is not known for certain, Downy Woodpeckers may also engage in a type of foraging behavior called traplining, which involves visiting a series of good foraging locations in a sequential and systematic way. For downies, traplining would require a good memory of the relative locations of particular snags and trees in their territories.

4

Drumming, Tapping, and Communication

Woodpeckers are unique among birds in producing sounds by striking their bills against wood or other substrates. These sounds, variously referred to as drumming, tattooing, tapping, and rapping, are used to communicate with members of the same species. Sounds are also produced when woodpeckers are foraging or excavating cavities, but these are incidental sounds that generally play no role in communication. Woodpeckers can also communicate by producing sounds with the syrinx, as do other birds. The syrinx, unique to birds, is found deep in the chest at the point where the trachea, or windpipe, splits into the two primary bronchi. The syrinx possesses thin membranes that vibrate and thus create sound as air passes by them.

Downy Woodpeckers, both males and females, use a variety of substrates for drumming, ranging from solid wood to hollow wood to, occasionally, downspouts, gutters, and antennas. A good resonant substrate, like a dead or hollow limb, is preferred because these substrates produce louder drums that carry greater distances. During a typical drum, downies hit the substrate at a rate of about sixteen or seventeen times per second, with an interval between successive hits of about 0.06 second. Drums can vary in duration from about 0.25 second (five hits) to 1.8 seconds (twenty-eight hits).

The drums of female downies are similar to those of males. The drums of different individuals within a population may differ in the average number of hits per drum, hit rate (number of hits per second), and duration. Such differences could potentially permit downies to recognize particular individuals by the characteristics of their drums, but because other characteristics of drums, like volume and pitch, vary with the type of substrate and the force with which the substrate is hit, individual recognition may often be difficult or impossible.

In fact, it appears that in some cases Downy Woodpeckers are unable to even determine what species of woodpecker is drumming. Downies coexist with several other species of woodpeckers that also drum. Although drums may differ among species, characteristics of drums of different woodpecker species sometimes overlap. As a result, drumming by an individual of one species sometimes elicits a response from individuals of another species. For example, downies may investigate a drumming Red-bellied Woodpecker, and vice versa. The approaching bird, however, upon hearing more species-specific vocalizations or making visual contact, will soon realize the mistake and move away.

Downies and other woodpeckers show distinct preferences for certain drumming sites, favored because of their resonant qualities. To enhance the distance the acoustic signals are transmitted, drumming posts are often located high in trees. Higher sites also provide drumming downies with a better view of the surrounding area and a better chance of observing intruding individuals, mates, or potential mates. Downies looking for drumming posts may tap or trial drum on prospective sites to determine their resonant quality. Those selected are often dead or hollow branches because such sites resonate more than live branches.

Downy Woodpeckers drum primarily from February through July, with little or no drumming during late summer, fall, and early winter. There is also daily variation in drumming behavior, with downies more likely to drum during the morning than during the afternoon or evening. Females drum as much as males. Drumming rates are generally higher just prior to nesting (March and April), lower during nesting (May and early June), higher again after young leave the nest (June), then lower again in July before drumming essentially ceases in August. Downies that lose mates during the breeding season drum at higher rates than downies that are paired.

What induces downies to initiate drumming as the breeding season approaches? It may not be a coincidence that drumming begins as days are becoming longer. Downies, like other birds, have special light receptors in the brain, and these receptors are stimulated by the longer days of January and February. Although not yet demonstrated in woodpeckers, in many other birds an area of the brain called the hypothalamus responds to increasingly long days by releasing hormones that stimulate the pituitary gland. In males, the pituitary then releases hormones that stimulate the testes. The testes respond by increasing in size and releasing increasing amounts of the hormone testosterone. This hormone then stimulates the growth of areas in the brain that control vocal behavior, and as a result, birds begin to sing. This may work similarly to induce drumming in downies.

Downy Woodpeckers drum, at varying rates, over a period of about six months. The use of this signal over such an extended period suggests that drumming serves a variety of functions. One such function is to aid in the establishment and maintenance of a breeding territory. Thus, to other downies of the same sex, drumming serves as a long-range keep-out signal. At shorter range, drumming near a member of the same sex probably signals aggression. When recordings of drums are played over a speaker in a downy's territory, simulating the presence of a drumming intruder, the resident typically responds in an aggressive manner, approaching, often very quickly, and sometimes drumming in response. Downies may also fly close to the speaker and vocalize, often giving whinny calls. The aim of this response is to evict the intruder from the territory.

Drumming may also serve to attract mates. As the breeding season approaches, unpaired downies drum at higher rates and with greater volume than downies with mates, and during the breeding season, downies that lose mates to predators do the same. The increased rate and volume of drumming serve to announce a downy's unpaired status, and unpaired downies in the vicinity may, in response, approach and may decide to pair with the signaling individual.

Beyond its role in territory defense and mate attraction, drumming by male downies may also serve other functions. A study in Kentucky revealed that male downies may drum at higher rates during the excavation of nest cavities and during the period just before females begin egg laying. Such timing suggests that drumming by male woodpeckers, like the singing of male songbirds, may serve to stimulate females. Alternatively, drumming by male downies during excavation and egg laying may represent mate guarding. During this time, female downies are fertile, and males may drum at higher rates to prevent other males from approaching, and potentially copulating with, their mates.

Drumming is also used by paired downies to maintain contact. As a pair of downies forage in different parts of their territory, each may drum occasionally to inform the other of its location. Sometimes paired downies drum at the same time or alternately. This is called duet drumming, and beyond providing information about location, such duetting may promote pairing and strengthen pair-bonds.

Male and female downies sometimes drum when seeking to copulate. Such solicitation often occurs near a pair's nest cavity. In the absence of its mate, a male or female wishing to copulate may drum near the cavity, and often the other bird, upon hearing the drumming, will fly to its mate and copulate.

Male and female Downy Woodpeckers also engage in tapping. As when drumming, downies strike their bills against a tree trunk or branch but do so at a relatively slow rate. During a typical tapping bout, downies tap nine or ten times at a rate of about three or four taps per second (compared with sixteen or seventeen hits per second when drumming). Downies tap in a variety of contexts, but in most cases, the tapping is not used to communicate with other downies. Downies most often tap when feeding, although such tapping is simply incidental to obtaining food.

Louise de Kiriline Lawrence studied woodpeckers for many years at her home in Pimisi Bay, Ontario, and suggested that tapping by woodpeckers may, on occasion, represent displacement behavior. Such behaviors are ones that occur out of context, often when two incompatible tendencies are activated at the same time, and they serve no apparent function. A bird engaged in an aggressive encounter may suddenly stop and begin to preen, suggesting a conflict between tendencies to continue the interaction and retreat. Similarly, as described by Lawrence, "a hungry woodpecker arrives at the feeding station and finds all the feeders occupied. The bird is by . . . rank not able to 'supplant' anyone feeding there. But its desire for food is compelling, and while waiting for its chance at a feeder it relieves its pent-up tension by tapping." It is also possible that such tapping serves to inform other downies of an individual's desire to avoid an aggressive interaction.

Tapping as a means of communication occurs infrequently, and almost always at a potential nest site. Either a male or female may begin tapping. This attracts the attention of the bird's mate and, if successful, informs the mate about the location of the potential nest site. The tapping may also provide important information about the quality of the wood at the site. If tapping fails to attract a mate, downies may begin to hit the substrate at a faster rate, called drum-tapping, or may begin to drum.

Another form of nonvocal communication among many woodpeckers, including downies, is wing rustling. This is a noise made by the wings, and it is apparently only produced under certain circumstances. Downies may wing rustle when flying from a foraging site after being disturbed by a potential predator, perhaps as a warning or alarm signal to a nearby mate. They may also wing rustle when approaching a nest cavity, possibly as a signal to an incubating or brooding mate or to nestlings. Such a signal would prepare those inside the cavity for the visit and permit a more rapid and efficient exchange, if an approaching bird is seeking to relieve an incubating or brooding mate, or transfer of food to nestlings.

Downy Woodpeckers use the syrinx to produce a variety of calls, each serving a different function. Among the most frequently uttered calls is the *pick* call, also referred to as the *pik*, *pit*, *chip*, *teak*, or *kick* call. It is very short in duration (about 0.035 second) and extends over a broad range of frequencies (2,000 to 4,000 hertz or cycles per second). These calls are given throughout the year and in a variety of contexts.

Pick calls are given by both males and females and sometimes function as location calls, with members of a pair giving these calls to inform a mate of their location. This call is often given by downies during, or shortly after, changes in position. In thick vegetation, where maintaining visual contact may be difficult if not impossible, such calls help a pair stay together. Also, adult downies sometimes utter *pick* calls as they approach a nest cavity. These calls may indicate that a nest visit is imminent and permit the nestlings to be ready. Such previsit communication may permit a more efficient, faster exchange. Less time at the nest may translate into more time foraging and a reduced likelihood that a predator will be alerted to the presence of the nest.

Pick calls also appear to indicate mild alarm. When a potential predator is spotted in the territory, downies may utter *pick* calls. This could serve to inform a mate or fledglings that a potential predator is nearby and increase their chances of avoiding predation. By varying the volume of *pick* calls and the number uttered, downies can provide more precise information. For example, double calls—two *picks* given in quick succession—indicate an increased level of alarm and a greater threat to a nearby mate or young and also inform the potential predator that it has been spotted. Double calls may also be given during aggressive, territorial interactions with other downies.

A related call given by Downy Woodpeckers is the *tickirr* call, also referred to as the *chrr*, *tichrr*, or short rattle call. It consists of a rapid series of *chip*-like notes. *Tickirr* calls are sometimes given during close interactions with other downies, suggesting an aggressive function. For example, downies have been heard giving *tickirrs* while aggressively chasing other downies. *Tickirr* calls also function as alarm calls, with downies using these calls to warn mates, nestlings, or fledglings of a potential predator, such as a hawk. Downies give these alarm calls only when near a mate or young. If foraging in a mixed-species flock that does not include another woodpecker, downies will not give alarm calls. Thus, downies clearly give these calls to protect mates or, during the breeding season, their young, possibly at some risk to themselves, because downies giving these calls may be revealing their location to potential predators.

Interestingly, other members of the mixed-species flocks that downies sometimes join, particularly chickadees and titmice, give their alarm calls much more frequently than downies, even in the absence of other members of their species. This may be because these

small, agile birds are unlikely to be captured by predators, and as a result, there is little risk involved in giving alarm calls. Downy Woodpeckers recognize the alarm calls of these other species and respond to them by remaining motionless, just as they do when they hear one of their own species give the *tickirr* call. This reduces the chances that they will be spotted by a nearby predator. In mixed-species flocks, therefore, chickadees and titmice function as lookouts or sentinels. As a result, other flock members, including Downy Woodpeckers, can spend less time looking for predators and more time foraging.

One of the more frequently uttered calls of Downy Woodpeckers is the whinny call, also known as the rattle or sputter call. This call sounds a bit like the whinny of a small horse. The whinny is uttered with more volume than other downy vocalizations, and it is estimated that it may be heard as far as a quarter mile away. Whinnies are about 1.5 seconds in duration and usually consist of ten to twenty-five notes that resemble *pick* calls. The first few notes of whinny calls are slightly higher in frequency and louder than the remaining notes. Whinnies are given by both males and females, primarily during late winter and early spring.

As with other Downy Woodpecker vocalizations, whinny calls serve more than one function. One likely is to inform a mate of a calling bird's location. *Pick* calls are also used as location calls, but over shorter distances. Whinnies are easier to locate over greater distances, because of the repetition of notes, and help keep mates aware of each other's location, even when some distance apart.

Whinny calls are also used to defend territories. A Downy Woodpecker may utter whinny calls when other downies trespass into its territory. Even simulated trespassing into a territory, such as playing taped drums or whinnies over a loudspeaker in a downy's territory, will elicit whinny calls.

A very low-volume call given infrequently by downies is referred to as the *chirr* or *tut-tit-wi-tut-it* call. This call is given during the breeding season when members of a mated pair approach each other. A pair of downies will sometimes give *chirr* calls at a nest when one individual is leaving and the other arriving. The function of this call is unclear, but it may help to reaffirm the pair-bond.

Another infrequently heard vocalization of Downy Woodpeckers is the *kweek* or *queek* call. These calls are given during courtship, often during courtship flights, and appear to play a role in the formation of pair-bonds.

Downy Woodpeckers also shriek or scream when held by a human or when captured and held by a predator. Shrieks are usually about 0.15 to 0.3 second in duration and may be given either singly or, more often, in series. These are also very high-volume calls with acoustic features that make them easy to locate. Similar calls are emitted by many other birds, and by some mammals as well, and there has been much speculation over their possible function. Other Downy Woodpeckers rarely respond vigorously to these distress screams. However, other predators are sometimes attracted. Thus, it is likely that these screams are meant to attract other, perhaps larger, predators, which, in their attempts to take the calling bird from the original predator, may permit the caller to escape. In fact, many studies have revealed that predators, including Downy Woodpecker

predators such as Sharp-shinned Hawks and Cooper's Hawks, are attracted to distress screams. Certainly, the likelihood that a screaming downy will escape from a predator is low, but it is not zero. Thus, screaming is probably a better strategy than remaining silent.

Young Downy Woodpeckers also use several types of calls. Like adults, juveniles utter screams when handled or captured by potential predators, and they probably do so for the same reasons. In addition, juveniles utter begging calls. These calls help adults monitor the hunger levels of their young, and after young fledge, the calls help the adults locate them. At hatching, young Downy Woodpeckers utter soft *pip-pip-pip* calls, also called chirp calls, plus longer, rasping notes. With increasing nestling age, these *pip* calls become longer in duration and louder and are referred to as squeak calls, or *tchick* calls. *Pip* and squeak calls are given by nestlings, especially older ones, during periods between visits by adults. The rasping call is given by nestlings soliciting food from an adult that has arrived at the nest. By the time of fledging, and continuing for several weeks thereafter, young downies continue to utter squeak calls to elicit feeding from adults. These calls probably provide adults with information about the hunger levels and location of fledglings.

Although many avian signals are vocal, birds also use a variety of visual displays. Some of these displays are used primarily during courtship, whereas others are used in aggressive contexts.

One Downy Woodpecker display has been referred to as the crest-raising display. Though downies do not have a true crest, they do erect the feathers on the top and back of the head during this display. Males perform this display more often than females, often during aggressive interactions with other males. Male downies performing this display are increasing the visibility of their red patch, and this probably signals increased aggression. Crest raising, by both males and females, often occurs in association with other displays.

Downies also use a bill-waving, or head-swinging, display. This display also signals aggression and is used in both male-male and female-female interactions. During this display, two downies face each other holding up their heads and bills and moving them from side to side. The distance and speed of swinging, plus the extent to which the head and bill are held up, vary with the level of aggression. Downies conveying a high level of aggression hold the head and bill down and do not swing back and forth very far. Downies signaling in this fashion may soon initiate an actual attack. Less aggressive, more submissive downies hold the head and bill high, swing back and forth over a wide arc, and are less likely to attack. These aggressive interactions are usually brief, with the submissive downy flying off to avoid conflict, although, rarely, these head-swinging bouts can continue off and on for an hour or more. Prolonged bouts are more likely to occur early in the breeding season when territory boundaries are being established.

During these intense, prolonged aggressive encounters, downies may extend both wings and spread the tail in a full wing-threat display, also called the wing-spreading display. While so displaying, a downy may also hop toward the other individual to signal greater aggression.

During an aggressive encounter between two equally matched downies, neither individual exhibits submission, and the encounter may escalate. One Downy Woodpecker may fly directly at the other, with the aggressor supplanting, or usurping the perch of, the other downy. Such supplanting attacks may occur several times. The supplanted individual may fly away, with the aggressor following and chasing.

Downy Woodpeckers also have a flutter aerial display, used primarily during and just prior to the breeding season. It is an aerial version of the wing-spreading display. One downy flies over or toward another downy, often landing near and sometimes supplanting the other bird. In flight, downies may either glide with wings held out or flap the wings in an exaggerated manner. This exaggerated flight has been described as batlike or mothlike. The flutter aerial display appears to be used primarily during pair formation by male and, less frequently, female downies. This display provides a good look at a displaying bird's plumage, particularly the wings, and therefore may provide prospective mates with information about the physical condition of the displaying individual. Some observers have suggested that this display can, at times, also be used in aggressive contexts.

Female Downy Woodpeckers indicate their readiness to copulate with a male by giving a copulatory display. During this display, a female may fly toward a male and perch crosswise or lengthwise on a horizontal branch. Once perched, the female holds its head and tail up and drops its wings slightly. With the tail up, the cloacal opening, where sperm are introduced by the male, is exposed. The male typically responds by flying toward and sometimes hovering briefly above the female. The male then lands on the lower back of the female, and copulation occurs.

5

Behavior

Birds that occupy forest habitats must fly through areas with a lot of branches and leaves. Although they provide a little less lift, shorter wings are favored in wooded areas because they improve maneuverability and make it easier for birds to avoid all the potential obstacles. Downy Woodpeckers are typically found in areas with lots of trees and thus have wings with a relatively low aspect ratio (the ratio of wing length to width). These wings serve downies very well because most flights are short and are often through relatively dense vegetation.

Downies, like most other woodpeckers, do not fly in a straight line but alternately rise and fall. These undulations occur because downies in flight flap their wings intermittently. Typically, downies rise as they flap their wings about six times (in about half a second), then fall as they pull their wings in against the body (for about a third of a second). This type of flight, during which downies achieve a speed of about 20 miles per hour, probably requires a bit less energy than continuous flapping flight, because friction with the air, or drag, is reduced slightly during the time when the wings are pulled in against the body.

As with wings, the legs and feet of birds vary with habitat and lifestyle. Downy Woodpeckers spend most of their time clinging to the trunks and branches of trees, and their legs and feet differ from those of most other birds. Most birds have legs and feet adapted for perching upright—relatively long legs and feet, with three toes projecting forward and one backward. Downies, in contrast, have relatively short legs and what ornithologists call zygodactyl feet—two toes projecting forward and two backward. At the end of each toe is a sharp, curved nail. Downies, therefore, can spread their toes and get a firm grip on almost any vertical, or nearly vertical, surface.

Downy Woodpeckers also use their tails for support when clinging to or climbing on a vertical trunk or limb. Bracing the tail against the bark is advantageous for woodpeckers because it reduces the amount of effort or energy needed to climb or cling. The tail helps support the weight of a woodpecker, and as a result, the leg muscles don't have to work as hard. The tail feathers—specifically, the shafts of the feathers—of downies and other woodpeckers can support this weight because they are very stiff compared with the tail feathers of other birds.

When climbing up a trunk or branch, downies first pull themselves toward the trunk, using their leg muscles, then basically hop upward. Both feet are held close together and move in unison. Their short legs keep downies close to the trunk or branch and thus make climbing easier.

Downies, like other birds, are covered with feathers, which serve many functions. They provide the streamlining needed for flight, and wing feathers provide both lift and propulsion. Feathers also protect a bird's skin and can play an important role in the maintenance of body temperature. Feather color often provides information needed to identify a bird's species, sex, and age. Feathers may also provide camouflage.

To serve these functions, a downy's feathers must be kept in good condition. Once fully developed, feathers are dead structures with no internal system of nourishment or maintenance. Downy Woodpeckers keep their feathers in good condition by preening. While preening, a downy may use its bill to apply secretions from its uropygial, or preen, gland. These oily secretions contain a mixture of waxes, fatty acids, fat, and water. They help preserve feather moistness and flexibility and may also help protect feathers from bacteria and fungi. Preening downies also remove feather parasites.

Among the external parasites, known as ectoparasites, potentially living in or on the feathers and skin of Downy Woodpeckers are chewing lice and louse flies. Chewing lice may feed on feathers, skin, or blood, depending on the species. Louse flies, also called hippoboscid flies, are flat flies that live among bird feathers and suck blood. Increased numbers of these and other parasites can have a detrimental effect on downies, due to loss of blood and damage to feathers, and thus regular preening is very important.

Downy Woodpeckers are rarely observed bathing. Downies bathe occasionally during periods of rain, but do not appear to regularly bathe in pools of water on the ground or in birdbaths. When downies do take baths, such behavior serves to remove dust, dirt, and parasites from feathers.

Downies occasionally sunbathe. One obvious reason for such behavior is to absorb solar radiation, which helps a bird maintain its body temperature on cold days. Sunbathing may also help downies eliminate feather parasites. The heat generated by solar radiation may cause parasites to move, and a preening woodpecker can then more easily locate and remove them.

Downy Woodpeckers roost and sleep in cavities throughout the year. Only if no cavities are available, as might be the case when young first disperse from their parents' territory into new areas, would a downy roost outside a cavity. Cavities offer two important advantages for Downy Woodpeckers, providing protection from predators and from the elements.

Downy Woodpeckers may excavate new roosting cavities at any time of year but do most of their excavation during the fall months and prior to the onset of winter. Roosting cavities are typically excavated over a period of about a week, but excavation time can be as short as three or four days if a new cavity is needed and no others are available. The time needed to excavate a cavity also varies with the consistency of the wood. Downies require more time to excavate cavities in

the harder wood of live trees than in the softer wood of snags or dead branches.

Cavities can be anywhere from 5 to 60 feet above the ground but are usually about 7 to 20 feet high. These heights are probably best because very low cavities would be more accessible to ground-dwelling predators, and very high cavities would be more exposed to wind, rain, and snow. Recent studies suggest that females may excavate cavities a bit lower in trees than males. If so, this may be a means by which paired downies avoid competition for good cavity sites.

Downies excavate cavities in snags, in dead limbs of live trees, or, less often, in live trees. Trees in which downies excavate roost cavities are usually 6 to 12 inches in diameter, but smaller or larger trees are sometimes used. A potential disadvantage of excavating a cavity in a small tree is that the presence of the cavity creates a weak point that could break during a storm. Cavity entrances are often just large enough to permit a downy to pass through. This is beneficial, because a small entrance more effectively excludes potential predators and cavity competitors. The length of the entrance tunnel varies with the diameter of the tree or limb but is typically several inches long. At the end of this tunnel, the cavity then goes down about 6 to 10 inches. The bottom of the cavity is generally a bit narrower than the top.

Downies apparently prefer to use trees that are not too close to other large trees. Predators, particularly large ones like raccoons, could potentially climb nearby trees to gain access to a downy's cavity, so excavating a cavity in a relatively small tree with no large trees nearby may reduce the risk of predation.

Cavities are usually oriented away from prevailing winds. In addition, downies sometimes construct cavities in trees or snags that are leaning slightly. On such trees, downies usually excavate the cavity on the side leaning toward the ground, unless the tree is leaning in the direction of the prevailing winds. Orienting cavity entrances away from prevailing winds and toward the ground is valuable, particularly during the winter, because temperatures in cavities will remain a bit higher if wind and precipitation don't blow directly into the cavity.

Downy Woodpeckers actively defend their roost cavities from other downies and, occasionally, other species. Such defense is not surprising, because downies invest much time and energy in excavating cavities, and particularly during cold weather, a downy without a roost cavity may be less likely to survive. Several other species, including chickadees, Tufted Titmice, and White-breasted Nuthatches, as well as flying squirrels, like to roost in cavities and will sometimes take over a downy's cavity. The downy may be able to reclaim the cavity at a later date but sometimes must use other cavities (downies may construct more than one roost cavity) or excavate a new one.

Other species of woodpeckers may also usurp downy roost cavities. Larger species, like Hairy and Red-bellied Woodpeckers, sometimes enlarge Downy Woodpecker cavities for their own use. Once so enlarged, downies generally will not use the cavities.

Downy Woodpeckers maintain territories in which all important activities take place, including mating, nesting, and feeding. These territories are actively defended only during the breeding season, generally beginning in February or March and extending through August or September. The size of these territories varies with habitat quality and population density but generally ranges from 2 to 10 hectares (4.5 to 25 acres).

Territories are defended primarily by males. Female Downy Woodpeckers do not defend territories as vigorously as males, although they do chase intruding females from their territories, especially if those females come near their mates or nests.

Male downies begin to drum in February or March, and chases among males become more frequent. During this time, males gradually range over smaller areas and begin to defend these areas with increasing vigor. Territories are established by drumming as well as through displays, chases, and fights. Males often establish territories in the same area year after year. In areas with high densities of males, territory boundaries may be very well defined. With decreasing densities, boundaries may become less precise. Boundaries may also fluctuate during the breeding season. One factor contributing to such fluctuation may be the location of the nest cavity. During nesting, male activity is centered at the nest, and as a result, boundaries some distance from nests may not be defended as vigorously. Neighboring males may then extend their territories variable distances into these less well defended areas.

The vigor of territory defense declines during the breeding season, as downies direct their attention and efforts to other activities, such as feeding nestlings or fledglings. As the breeding season ends, generally by September, the intensity of territory defense declines still further, and trespassing by other Downy Woodpeckers occurs more frequently. Because defense of boundaries is less vigorous or even nonexistent during the nonbreeding season, the areas occupied by downies during this time are best referred to as home ranges rather than territories. As a result of this reduced aggression, the winter ranges of downies, especially those of males and females, overlap.

Although the boundaries of ranges are not defended during the nonbreeding season, some aggression may still occur, because downies do vigorously defend their roosting cavities. Males and females defend roosting cavities, as well as an area of variable size around cavities, with equal vigor, and this aggression can be directed against other downies as well as other species.

6

The Breeding Season

Throughout much of the eastern United States, the breeding season of Downy Woodpeckers extends from February through July. During February, March, and April, male downies establish territories and seek mates. Actual nesting usually begins sometime during April or May, and young usually fledge by June or July. Excavation of nest cavities typically begins in mid- to late April. The nesting season begins a bit sooner for downies in the southern portion of their range and somewhat later in Canada and Alaska.

Studies of other bird species indicate that age influences the timing of reproduction. Typically, older individuals begin breeding before younger individuals, particularly before first-time breeders. Several factors may contribute to the later initiation of breeding by first-year birds. First, young males must establish territories and, when attempting to do so, are usually at a competitive disadvantage. Older male downies usually remain in or near their territories from previous years and, as the breeding season begins, can quickly reestablish dominance in their former territories. Younger males may have to move around looking for open territories and, as a result, often establish territories later than the older, established males. Similarly, older downies can often form pairs before first-year birds because they may pair up with their mates from the previous year, and re-forming a pair-bond takes less time than forming a new pair-bond.

A third possible factor might be differences in physical condition. Older birds, which have more experience and are better at locating food, tend to forage more efficiently than first-year birds. As a result, they may be in better physical condition and have larger energy reserves than younger birds. Because many reproductive activities, such as defending a territory or producing a clutch of eggs, require the expenditure of substantial amounts of energy, older birds can start breeding before the younger ones. Starting earlier is advantageous. Studies of a number of species show that earlier breeders are more successful, producing more young, and those young are more likely to survive. Young from earlier broods have more time to develop their skills, including foraging skills, than young from later broods. These older juveniles will usually be able to dominate less experienced young from later nests and, therefore, will be more likely to survive.

During the nesting season, pairs of Downy Woodpeckers usually raise just one brood. Although downies whose nests are lost during incubation or when nestlings are just a few days old will often attempt to nest again, downies rarely, if ever, attempt to raise a second brood after a first brood fledges. This is likely because downies have a relatively long nesting cycle, and there simply isn't enough time to raise more than one brood during a single breeding season.

Downy Woodpeckers, like many other excavators or primary cavity nesters, have relatively high nesting success, meaning that at least one young fledges from a nest. Nesting

success for birds like downies that excavate their own cavities is usually about 70 to 85 percent. By comparison, nesting success for secondary cavity nesting species—those that do not excavate their own cavities but use those created by primary cavity nesters—is typically about 55 to 65 percent, and nesting success for open-nesting species is usually even lower. Cavity nesters, both primary and secondary, tend to have higher nesting success than open nesters because predators are less likely to locate nests in cavities than open nests. And even if a predator does detect a cavity nest, the diameter of the entrance hole may prevent entry.

Although Downy Woodpecker nests are usually successful, some are lost to predators. Possible nest predators vary with location but may include tree-climbing snakes, small mammals, foxes, gray and red squirrels, raccoons, and opossums. Little is known about factors that might influence predation rates on Downy Woodpecker nests. Snakes and small mammals can more easily access low nests, however, and it is likely that such nests suffer higher rates of predation. Also, predators can get to lower cavities faster, reducing the possibility that adults will detect and successfully defend the nest site. Cavities in trees or snags with a lot of deciduous foliage nearby are more likely to suffer predation because parents may have difficulty detecting and driving off approaching predators. Downy nests located in well-decayed snags are also more susceptible to predation, because cavities excavated in softer wood can be opened more easily by predators, particularly by larger ones like raccoons.

Although predation of eggs or nestlings is the primary cause of nest failure, some downy nests also fail as a result of natural causes. Cavity trees, snags, or branches sometimes break because the cavity has created a weak area, and nest trees or snags are sometimes blown down by high winds.

Most species of birds, including Downy Woodpeckers, are socially monogamous, forming prolonged pair-bonds with one member of the opposite sex. Male and female downies typically form pair-bonds that last for one entire breeding season, although they sometimes extend over two or more breeding seasons.

Most downies appear to form pair-bonds between February and early April. Older downies usually pair before younger ones, especially before first-year birds. Males and females paired to each other during previous breeding seasons are often the first to pair up as a new breeding season approaches, sometimes forming pairs as early as January. Such pairs probably remain near each other, with overlapping ranges, throughout the winter. During February, and continuing into March, males and females may seem to be associating with each other, but these early associations do not always result in pairing. As males begin to establish territories, females may temporarily associate with them, perhaps to examine the quality of a male, his territory, or both. If a female finds the male or his territory lacking, she may move to another male's territory.

The formation of a pair-bond begins with a male Downy Woodpecker establishing a territory. Males begin drumming more frequently, and one likely function of this drumming is to attract the attention of females. A female entering a male's territory may spend some time feeding and resting but eventually approaches the male's position. A male spotting a female in his territory may respond by flying toward her, perhaps displacing her, and sometimes performing a flutter aerial display. The female may fly as the male approaches, and if so, the male will typically fly after her. Such chases, after flutter aerial displays and at other times as well, may occur frequently during the first few days after a pair's initial encounter. A female attempting to perch after a chase is likely to be supplanted and chased once again. By remaining in a male's territory despite frequent chasing and supplanting, a female may be indicating her willingness to pair.

A male Downy Woodpecker descending toward a female during a flutter aerial display may be advertising his physical condition and, perhaps, the condition and quality of his plumage. During these flights, the male flies with wings and tail spread, apparently giving the female a good look at the plumage in these areas. The persistence of the male downy as he chases potential mates early in the pairing process may provide females with additional information about his physical condition.

Occasionally, female downies appear to take the initiative in pairing. As described by Louise de Kiriline Lawrence, females may announce their presence "by drumming, thus establishing long-distance contact with the male. He hears the drumming and answers, whereupon the birds enter a stage of nonapproach. During this stage, while the birds travel over a large area, reciprocal drumming plays a major role. This drumming exchange . . . seem[s] to have a highly stimulating effect, especially on the male. He approaches the female and displays at close quarters. The female soon demonstrates her response by a show of rising interest in old nest holes and possible nest sites. By following each other about, by their displays to each other . . . and their search of suitable nest sites, the birds gradually begin to synchronize their behavior. And eventually the teamwork between the sexes that plays so important a part in the nesting success of the woodpeckers is established."

During courtship, male and female Downy Woodpeckers occasionally duet. During duets, males and females engage in reciprocal drumming, with one drumming and then the other. Such drumming may provide information about each bird's location and help members of a pair maintain contact with each other. These duets may help strengthen the pair-bond. A member of a pair may also drum to encourage its mate to inspect a potential nest site.

After pairing, duetting may serve somewhat different functions. A female may drum with her mate to advertise her presence and, simultaneously, the mated status of her mate. Such behavior may be important in mate retention, because other females in the area may still be looking for mates. This advertising may reduce the chances that other females will enter a female's territory seeking a mate, but some trespassing is still likely to occur. In response, mated females will attempt to drive female trespassers from their territories. These interactions may involve vigorous chasing and, less commonly, physical contact and fighting. Lawrence described one such intrusion into the territory of a downy pair by a female apparently looking for a mate. In response, the resident female "abandoned wing-flapping and other gestures of lesser intensity. With her immaculate breast and the white lining of her wide-opened wings fully exposed, she rose high on her feet and with her whole body performed a fantastic wobbling display. Thus teetering atop the branch, she looked like a small windmill. To this [the intruding female] responded with vigor . . . [and] wave upon wave of female attack, pursuit, and wobbling display surged back and forth. The females several times came together in brief clashes and downy feathers drifted lightly upon the air."

Courtship among downies, as in many other species of birds, often appears to be a case of females choosing from available males. Females may, however, occasionally, take the initiative. Courtship typically requires a substantial investment in time and energy by males. Male downies must obtain and defend a territory, drum to attract potential mates, then impress visiting females with drums, flights, displays, and, perhaps, potential nest sites. Females choose or reject males based on the quality of a male's territory, specifically, foraging sites and potential nesting sites, drumming, plumage, and vigor of display. Male downies deficient in any of these may have difficulty obtaining or keeping a mate.

Lawrence Kilham, who has studied various aspects of woodpecker behavior and ecology for more than thirty-five years, once monitored a pair of downies in a young forest in New Hampshire where there were no suitable nest sites. He noted that the pair "inspected every possible stub in their territories in vain." Shortly thereafter, the female of this pair apparently divorced the male and sought better luck, and perhaps a better male, elsewhere.

7

Nest Building, Egg Laying, and Incubation

Downy Woodpeckers excavate a new cavity for each nesting attempt. Before the initiation of breeding, the male and female visit several potential nest sites. These potential sites can be located along the edges of wooded areas or in dense stands of forest some distance from any openings. Although either sex may select a nest site, the female often appears to make the final decision. When a potential site is located, a downy may drum to inform its mate. The mate may then approach, while the downy at the site taps several times before flying off. The arriving mate then examines the site and may drum or tap as part of the evaluation process. Potential sites may be inspected several times before being accepted or rejected. Sometimes downies begin excavating at several sites before one site is finally chosen. One investigator observed a pair of downies in which the male and female disagreed about the choice of a nest site and each began excavating at a different site. Each inspected the other's site, but the two birds failed to agree that one site was better. As a result, both sites were abandoned and another site chosen.

Downy Woodpeckers excavate nest cavities in a variety of different trees, including aspens, cottonwoods, willows, elms, oaks, ashes, and snags of many kinds. Downies often excavate cavities in trees showing signs of decay—ones with broken tops or large, broken branches. The presence of decay, caused by fungal infections, softens the wood and makes excavation easier. This may be particularly important for downies, because their small size and small bills make excavating in live wood difficult. Before initiating excavation, downies tap or drum at the prospective site, probably to determine the quality and soundness of the underlying wood.

Downies usually select excavation sites about 15 to 20 feet above the ground, although entrances to nest cavities may range from as low as 8 feet to as high as 50 feet. Trees or snags

in which downies excavate nest cavities are usually about 10 to 15 inches in diameter (measured about 4 feet above the ground) and 20 to 35 feet in height. The diameter of trees, branches, or snags at the cavity entrance is often about 5 to 7 inches. Some studies also suggest that downies prefer to excavate nest cavities in areas with somewhat smaller trees and more understory vegetation than other, larger species of woodpeckers. Downies may prefer smaller trees to avoid the difficulty of excavating through the thicker sapwood of larger trees, and understory vegetation may be beneficial because downies often forage on small trees and shrubs.

Male and female downies generally work together when excavating nest cavities, although the division of labor varies among pairs. In some pairs, males do more of the excavating; in others, females do more. Once excavation begins, downies usually need about sixteen days to complete the work, although the time required to excavate a nest cavity may range anywhere from about seven to twenty days.

At least two factors contribute to differences in the time required to excavate a cavity. One is the relative hardness of the wood. Excavating a cavity in softer wood, like that of some snags, requires less time than does excavating a cavity in a live tree with harder wood. Also, it may be beneficial to complete cavities close to the time that egg laying will begin, because such timing probably reduces the chances of losing a completed cavity to a nest-site competitor. Thus, when a site is chosen well before egg laying, excavation may proceed at a relatively slow pace, whereas sites located shortly before egg laying may be excavated much faster.

Most excavation occurs during the morning. When a cavity must be completed quickly, however, work may continue into the afternoon and evening. If a nearly completed cavity is lost to a nest-site competitor shortly before a female is to begin egg laying, a pair of downies may work throughout the day to complete a new cavity as quickly as possible.

Excavation of a nest cavity begins with the formation of an entrance tunnel. This is followed by creation of a curved link between the tunnel and the main part of the cavity. Finally, the nesting chamber itself is excavated.

To start an excavation, downies use their bills to create a conelike depression at the center of what will soon be the cavity entrance. This depression is gradually made deeper and wider. When the opening is wide enough, downies are able to begin reaching in to make the cavity deeper. Typically, the diameter of the entrance hole is just large enough to permit a downy to squeeze through. Sawdust and wood chips produced as the early excavation process proceeds are usually gathered in the bill and simply tossed over the shoulder. Rarely, a downy flies from the excavation site with sawdust and wood chips in its bill and drops the material some distance away.

As downies complete the entrance tunnel and begin excavating downward, sometimes only the tail can be seen extending from the opening. At this stage, downies must back out of the cavity after a period of excavation. The small diameter of the cavity, combined with the need to overcome the additional friction created by backward-projecting feathers, can make this exit quite difficult, and downies sometimes must squirm and struggle to get out. During such exits, a downy's plumage may become disheveled, and a period of preening may be required.

As the excavation continues downward, downies also enlarge the inner diameter of the nest cavity. Once the cavity is a few inches deep, downies have enough room to turn around, and they begin to emerge headfirst. Inside the nest cavity, downies continue drilling downward and also work to enlarge the diameter of the actual nesting chamber. At this stage, downies can sometimes be heard as they pound and drill inside the cavity. While working on the inner walls, wood chips and sawdust fall to the bottom of the cavity. Excavating downies may take short breaks to throw out some of this material. Often, however, this material is left when an excavation session ends, and the next downy to work on the cavity (the mate

or the same bird after its break is over) removes some of the debris before continuing the excavation.

During a typical excavation, the time spent working on the cavity varies. During the first few days, downies spend relatively little time excavating and more time engaged in other activities, such as foraging. As the excavation process continues, downies spend progressively more time excavating. A downy may work on the cavity for as little as a few minutes at a time or, less frequently, as much as an hour or more, although typically a downy will work for fifteen to twenty minutes before taking a break and sometimes will be relieved by its mate.

Excavation often requires that male and female downies coordinate their activities. When one bird completes a period of excavation, its mate often takes over. It may also be important, particularly as the nest cavity nears completion, for at least one member of the pair to remain at or near the site to watch for potential nest-site competitors. Males and females communicate with each other during excavation, often using whinny calls and drums to stay in contact and perhaps to help coordinate their activities.

Completed cavities vary in size, but a typical nest chamber is 8 to 12 inches deep and about 3 inches in diameter at the top, narrowing to about 2 to $2^1/_2$ inches in diameter at the bottom. Downies do not carry any nesting material into the cavity, but the sawdust and wood chips at the bottom provide a soft cushion for the eggs and later, nestlings.

Because suitable nest sites or cavities may be in short supply, downies must often defend their cavities from other species. Larger species of woodpeckers, including Red-bellied Woodpeckers (top), Yellow-bellied Sapsuckers, Hairy Woodpeckers, and Northern Flickers, sometimes attempt to take over cavities that downies have excavated or have started to excavate. Downies will usually attempt to chase away these nest-site competitors, but sometimes these larger woodpeckers enlarge a cavity's entrance while the downies are absent, and the downies must then abandon the site.

Downies will also defend newly excavated cavities from a variety of secondary cavity nesters, including Red-breasted and White-breasted Nuthatches, Black-capped and Carolina Chickadees, and less frequently, Eastern Bluebirds, House Sparrows, and European Starlings. Starlings are particularly aggressive when attempting to usurp a cavity. Sometimes, as in the case of Downy Woodpecker cavities, even when the starling is too large to use the cavity, it may repeatedly try to enter it, thereby preventing the downies from using it.

Downy Woodpecker nest cavities represent containers for eggs and, later, nestlings, and these containers serve a variety of functions. One important function is to provide a suitable microclimate for the eggs, the nestlings, and the incubating or brooding adult. The nest microclimate, or temperature, must be different from the surrounding climate because eggs and young nestlings require temperatures that are warm but not too warm. In addition, the ability of a nest to retain heat can have a substantial effect on the energy that an incubating or brooding adult must expend.

The microclimate of a downy's nest cavity is likely influenced by the entrance hole's orientation and location. The entrances of downy cavities are often oriented away from the prevailing winds, and this may help maintain warmer temperatures within the cavity as well as reduce the likelihood that wind-blown rain will enter. The entrances to downy nest cavities are sometimes located on the undersides of branches or sloping trunks, and this may provide further protection from wind and rain.

As excavation of the nest cavity nears completion, and continuing until the day that the next to last egg is laid, female Downy Woodpeckers are fertile. Any sperm deposited in the female reproductive tract during this period may fertilize an egg. Among downies, this sperm almost always comes from a female's mate. For most downies, it simply may not pay to pursue copulations with downies other than their mates (extra-pair copulations). A male or female pursuing extra-pair copulations would have less time to excavate and guard cavities, incubate eggs, and brood and feed nestlings. Because both members of a pair play an important role in each of these activities, time spent doing other things, such as pursuing copulations with other downies, would likely reduce the chances of successful reproduction. So the best strategy for downies is to focus on raising their own young rather than seeking extra-pair copulations.

The function of copulation is to introduce a male's sperm into a female's reproductive tract. In male Downy Woodpeckers, sperm is produced in the testes. During the nonbreeding period, the testes do not produce sperm and are very small. As spring approaches and the ratio of daylight to dark increases, the longer days stimulate the pituitary gland to produce hormones that stimulate the testes, and the testes begin to increase in size and may eventually become four hundred to five hundred times larger. The increasingly large testes start producing the hormone testosterone, which causes male downies to begin establishing territories and drumming.

The reproductive tract of a female Downy Woodpecker consists of a single ovary containing several hundred to a thousand or more eggs plus an oviduct. The female reproductive tract, under the influence of pituitary hormones, also exhibits a tremendous increase in size as the breeding season approaches. As it increases in size, the ovary begins to produce the hormone estrogen, which stimulates the female to initiate pair-bonding and other reproductive behaviors. In both males and females, the pituitary also releases increasing amounts of a hormone called prolactin, which promotes development of a brood patch and stimulates the birds to incubate eggs and brood young.

Undeveloped eggs in the ovaries of female downies are microscopic, but by the time they are laid, they will have increased in size by as much as one thousand times. Part of this increase is the result of yolk deposition in the ovary. This yolk is important, because it provides energy for the developing downy. Before laying begins, the ovary contains several eggs at various stages of development. During the period of egg laying, an egg is released from the ovary, a process called ovulation, about every twenty-four hours, and this released egg then moves into the oviduct.

It is in the first section of the oviduct, called the infundibulum, that the egg must be fertilized by a male's sperm. Fertilization must occur here because, after leaving the infundibulum, the egg passes into an area called the magnum, where the albumen, or egg white, is added to the egg, and sperm cannot penetrate the albumen. Because the egg remains in the infundibulum for only about twenty to thirty minutes, the period of time when fertilization can occur is very short. So sperm must be present in the infundibulum during this critical period.

Sperm are transferred from male to female during copulation. Downies usually begin copulating as their nest cavity nears completion, and most copulations take place near the nest cavity. A female downy soliciting copulation perches crosswise, or occasionally lengthwise, on a horizontal limb. The female raises up on her legs, elevates her tail, and tilts her head back, with wings slightly drooping. With the tail up, the opening into the cloaca—and therefore into the female reproductive tract—is exposed. The nearby male may then move toward the female and mount her. Sometimes, however, the male downy leaves his perch, flies toward the female, and briefly hovers above her before landing on her lower back. The male then brings his cloacal opening into contact with hers in what is often described as a cloacal kiss. The male then ejaculates, releasing several hundred million sperm into the female's cloaca. During copulation, a male downy may use his wings to maintain his balance on top of the female. Copulation takes about ten to eighteen seconds, and both male and female may give low-volume call notes when so engaged.

Either sex may initiate copulation. Sometimes males and females drum to indicate their readiness. At other times, either the male or female will fly to a branch where the pair has copulated previously, and the nearby mate may respond by approaching and copulating.

Paired Downy Woodpeckers may begin copulating several weeks before egg laying begins, but most copulations occur during egg laying. Downies may copulate frequently, probably to help strengthen the pair-bond and help ensure successful fertilization.

Once deposited in the female's cloaca, sperm begin moving up the oviduct, and if no egg is present in the oviduct, some may reach the infundibulum within fifteen minutes. Not all sperm begin to move up the oviduct, however; some move into special sperm storage tubules located in the walls of the lower portion of the oviduct. Sperm may be stored in these tubules for several days or more and appear to be released continuously. Thus, females have a constant supply of sperm to fertilize eggs.

Copulatory behavior begins a week or even more before a female Downy Woodpecker lays her first egg and peaks two to five days before egg laying begins. Such timing may seem inappropriate, because eggs are available for fertilization during egg laying, not before. Once a female begins to lay, however, sperm are largely unable to make their way up the oviduct, because the way is blocked by an egg moving down the oviduct. During egg laying, female Downy Woodpeckers typically lay an egg every twenty-four hours. As a result, the only time that sperm are able to move up the oviduct is immediately after an egg has been laid. At this point, another egg will be ovulated and enter the infundibulum. So for about an hour or less after a female downy lays an egg, and assuming the clutch is not yet complete, introduced sperm have an open pathway up the oviduct. Because a male Downy Woodpecker may be engaged in other activities, such as foraging or defending the territory, and therefore may not be available to copulate with his mate during that short window of opportunity, the best strategy is probably to copulate with his mate as much as possible prior to egg laying and get sperm into her storage tubules. Then, some of the continuously released sperm from those

tubules will be in the infundibulum at the appropriate time and can fertilize the egg.

Once fertilized, the egg continues down the oviduct and passes into the magnum, where the albumen is deposited; through an area called the isthmus, where two membranes are added, an inner membrane that surrounds the albumen and an outer membrane; and finally, into the uterus, where the shell is formed over a period of about twenty hours.

Downy Woodpecker eggs are typically oval. The shell is smooth and white. Many cavity-nesting birds have white eggs, because there is no need for

camouflage in cavities, and the enhanced visibility of white eggs in a dark cavity may help prevent accidental breakage of the eggs by the parents. Downy eggs are about $4/5$ inch by $3/5$ inch (19.5 millimeters by 15 millimeters).

Female Downy Woodpeckers generally begin laying eggs a few days after the nest cavity is completed, but this interval may be anywhere from about one to ten days. Typically, females lay one egg per day, early in the morning, and eggs in a clutch are laid on successive days. Complete clutches usually consist of five eggs but may contain from three to eight. In some species, and perhaps in Downy Woodpeckers as well, female age also has an effect on clutch size, with young females laying fewer eggs than older ones. Although it is not always clear why older females produce larger clutches, one possibility is that older, more experienced females are better foragers and therefore are in better physical condition. Because egg production is energetically expensive, females in better condition are able to lay more eggs.

The brood patch, or incubation patch, is a bare, flaccid area of skin that covers much of the abdomen and part of the breast of both female and male Downy Woodpeckers. Feathers are lost in this area, and the area swells and softens. The patch is also highly vascular, with much blood flowing into the patch when a male or female is incubating eggs or brooding young. The loss of feathers plus the softening and swelling permit better contact between the skin and the eggs or young, and the blood delivers heat.

During incubation, which is the application of heat to eggs, male and female downies try to keep the eggs at a temperature of about 98 to 100 degrees F. Temperatures above 106

degrees F may kill developing embryos, between 78 and 94 degrees F can disrupt normal development, and below 78 degrees F may stop development. While incubating, downies periodically rotate and rearrange the eggs in the nest. This movement provides equal heating throughout each egg and also prevents the shell membranes from adhering to the shell, which could interfere with hatching.

Incubation is performed by both male and female Downy Woodpeckers, but only males incubate at night. During the day, adult downies typically incubate for thirty to sixty minutes before being relieved by a mate or taking a break. While incubating, the adult downy holds its wings close to the body and its tail slightly elevated. Incubating adults occasionally engage in other activities, including preening, sleeping, and turning the eggs. During breaks away from the nest, adult downies may defecate and also spend some time foraging. The incubation schedule is very flexible, with downies spending more time incubating during periods of cool weather or precipitation and less time during periods of very warm weather.

When a potential predator approaches a nest cavity with eggs, male and female Downy Woodpeckers will defend the nest site. Typically, the incubating adult moves to the cavity entrance and, if the predator reaches the entrance, will sometimes attempt to peck the intruder. The other adult, if nearby, may also assist in the defense effort by flying at the predator and vocalizing. Although adult downies often defend nest cavities containing eggs, defense typically becomes more vigorous after the eggs hatch.

The incubation period for Downy Woodpeckers is twelve days. In general, woodpeckers, including downies, have shorter incubation periods than most other birds of comparable size. Recently, investigators Yoram Yom-Tov and Amos Ar suggested that this represents an adaptation for breeding in cavities. Gas exchange in cavities may be poor, and oxygen concentrations near the bottom of the cavity may be low, especially at night, when the incubating adult doesn't leave the nest. During late incubation, when the needs of the developing embryos for oxygen increase, the poorly ventilated atmosphere at the bottom of the nest cavity may stress the embryos. A shorter incubation period would solve this problem, because the exchange of gases through eggshells is less efficient than exchange via lungs. In addition, after hatching, parents must feed nestlings and therefore make more trips into and out of the cavity. Such movements improve air circulation and elevate oxygen levels near the bottom of the cavity.

Embryos grow slowly for the first two or three days of incubation but then enter a period of rapid weight gain. The embryo's main systems—circulatory, digestive, respiratory, and nervous—begin to differentiate by the second or third day. Limb movements begin as early as the fourth day, and the egg tooth, a projection near the tip of the bill that helps the young woodpecker break through the shell, becomes apparent by the fifth or sixth day. As development proceeds, the yolk sac gets smaller as the embryo grows.

As the period of incubation comes to an end, the embryonic downy prepares for hatching. The embryo assumes a tucked position, with the head positioned so that the bill lies between the body and the right wing. A day or so before hatching, the young downy uses its bill to puncture the innermost shell membrane at the blunt end of the egg, a process referred to as internal pipping. At this location in the egg, there is a pocket of air between the inner and outer shell membrane that the young downy begins to breathe. After a few more hours, the young bird uses its egg tooth to break through the outer shell membrane and the shell, a process called external pipping. The young bird now begins to breathe fresh air from the outside. Over the next several hours, the young downy pecks the shell while slowly rotating, producing a small circle of cracks and holes. The chick then penetrates the shell at this circle and begins to emerge from the egg. Adults usually do not assist the young in the process of hatching. The young downy's egg tooth disappears by four days after hatching.

Adult Downy Woodpeckers usually don't begin prolonged incubation until after the clutch is complete, or nearly so. All eggs in a clutch normally hatch within twenty-four hours of each other, although at times the interval between hatching of the first and last eggs may be as long as forty-eight hours. On the day of hatching or during the next few days, adult downies may carry the shell fragments from the nest cavity and dispose of them, but they sometimes leave them in the cavity.

8

Nestlings and Their Parents

At hatching, young Downy Woodpeckers are naked, blind, and completely dependent on their parents. Young birds with these characteristics are referred to as altricial. (In contrast, precocial young, like those of ducks, grouse, and pheasants, are covered with down, have open eyes, and leave their nest soon after hatching.) Altricial young are also unable to maintain their body temperature. As a result, male and female downies must brood newly hatched nestlings, and during the first four to seven days after hatching, one of the parents nearly always remains at the nest. When brooding, the adult's brood patch is placed against the nestlings, thereby transferring heat to them. During the first two weeks after hatching, the amount of brooding varies with temperature. Adults brood less during warm weather and more during colder weather.

The ability of nestlings to produce their own heat and maintain a constant body temperature improves throughout the nestling period. At fledging, young downies maintain body temperature nearly as well as adults. Because older nestlings generate heat and maintain their body temperature reasonably well, adult downies spend only about 10 to 20 percent of their time brooding by nine or ten days after hatching. By fourteen days after hatching, adults rarely, if ever, brood young.

Males and females share brooding duties equally during the day, but males brood during the night. As with incubation, the advantage of sharing brooding duties is that, at least during the first several days after hatching, an adult is almost always present in the cavity, thus providing better defense of the nest cavity and nestlings. During the day, brooding periods vary in duration from just a few minutes to nearly an hour, averaging about ten minutes. These periods tend to become shorter as the nestling period progresses.

The time that adult downies spend brooding young also varies with brood size, with larger broods requiring less brooding than smaller broods. This is true because young huddled together in a nest have less skin surface exposed and lose heat at a slower rate, and more nestlings mean less exposed skin surface.

Nestlings also require food, and both adult downies feed nestlings, although the relative contributions of males and females may vary among pairs. At many nests, males and females contribute equally to feeding nestlings. In other cases male downies feed the nestlings more than females, particularly later in the nestling period. Nevertheless, in most pairs of Downy Woodpeckers, both parents contribute substantially to the feeding of nestlings. One possible reason for this is that adult downies share brooding duties. Because both male and female downies brood young, both can participate in feeding nestlings.

More important, both parents must feed the nestlings because one adult alone is probably not capable of maintaining the feeding rates necessary to fledge the entire brood. Observations of other woodpecker species suggest that the young usually do not survive to fledging if one of the parents is killed early in the nestling period. When one parent is killed, the other compensates by increasing its feeding rate. Unless its mate is killed late in the nestling period, however, the remaining parent is usually unable to maintain feeding rates at a sufficiently high level to successfully fledge the entire brood.

Editor's Note: A number of photographs in this chapter were taken by Harlo Hadow, Professor of Biology at Coe College, during a study of the growth and development of nestling Downy Woodpeckers. These photos show hand-held downies at various stages of development. The temporary removal of these nestlings from their nest was necessary for the study, and following the documentation of their day-to-day growth, the birds were left to fledge naturally in the wild. Holding birds in the hand is an activity best left to experts.

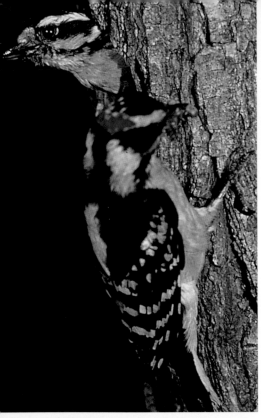

During the first few days after hatching, one of the parents is almost always at the nest. An adult arriving just outside a nest cavity may utter low-volume calls to inform the brooding mate of its arrival. Often, however, no vocalizations are given, and the brooding adult probably just hears its mate approach and land just outside the cavity. Either way, the brooding adult knows its mate has arrived and the exchange can take place. Later in the nestling period, when adults spend little time brooding, a downy's mate is unlikely to be in the cavity when it arrives, and no such exchanges are necessary.

Older, larger nestlings require more food to supply sufficient energy for temperature maintenance and for additional growth. Adults often increase feeding rates to meet the increasing demands of older nestlings. In addition to making more visits to the nest, adult downies may bring larger prey or more prey per visit as the nestling period progresses. Louise de Kiriline Lawrence monitored the provisioning behavior of three pairs of Downy Woodpeckers and noted that "the food seen in the bills . . . ranged from very small ants, one or two at a time, during the first days [after hatching] to enormous helpings of large-bodied insects that during the latter part of the nestling period protruded from all sides of the woodpeckers' bills."

Feeding rates may decline substantially as the end of the nestling period approaches. Low feeding rates mean that nestlings become increasingly hungry and increasingly active, eventually encouraging the young downies to fledge.

Adult Downy Woodpeckers with larger broods tend to bring food at somewhat higher rates. The increase in feeding rates is not proportional to the number of young to be fed, however, and as a result, individual nestlings in large broods receive less food than those in smaller broods. Nevertheless, nestlings in larger broods typically grow at the same rates as those in smaller broods, suggesting that nestlings in larger broods require less food. It may be that the energy needed to maintain normal body temperature is lower for nestlings in larger broods, because nestlings huddled together can share body heat, and each bird has less exposed body surface. Therefore, less energy—and less food—is needed to generate heat.

The manner in which adult downies deliver food to nestlings also changes during the nestling period. When nestlings are small, the adult enters the cavity, moves down headfirst toward the young while gripping the walls of the cavity with its feet, and then reaches down to deliver the food to one of its nestlings (only one nestling is fed per visit). After delivering the food, the adult downy turns around and, unless remaining to brood, leaves the cavity. By about ten days after hatching, nestlings are getting larger and reaching higher. The adult still enters the cavity headfirst but does not need to move down as far into the cavity, so at this stage, the very tip of the adult's tail may be visible just inside the cavity entrance. With larger nestlings, there is no longer room for the adult to easily turn around, so after delivering food, it backs out of the cavity. When fecal sacs must be removed, adults still completely enter the cavity.

By fifteen days or so after hatching, nestlings are even larger and may be able to climb up the inner walls of the cavity. At this stage, the adult may simply extend its head and neck into the cavity to feed a nestling. And beginning about five days before fledging, the adult need not even reach into the cavity, because nestlings move up to the entrance and extend their heads out in an attempt to obtain food.

When feeding nestlings, adults may forage in trees near the nest cavity, though they must sometimes travel to more distant sites. Good foraging sites located a reasonable distance from the nest cavity are important, because each adult may have to deliver food to nestlings every four to six minutes during the late nestling period. It is likely, therefore, that for most pairs, most foraging occurs within 300 to 400 feet of nest cavities, although one investigator observed an adult downy fly over 600 feet from the nest cavity to a foraging site.

The diet of nestling Downy Woodpeckers is entirely insects. Almost all nestling birds are fed insects, especially during the first few days after hatching. During this early nestling period, young birds grow rapidly. The production of new cells and tissues in these growing birds requires plenty of protein, and insects are richer in protein than plant materials.

Adult downies, as with many species of birds, bring their young small, soft-bodied prey such as caterpillars during the first two or three days after hatching. Soft-bodied larvae may be easier to digest than hard-bodied prey like beetles. The digestive systems of young birds may become more efficient with increasing age, permitting adults to provide older nestlings with more hard-bodied insect prey. To further help very young nestlings digest their food, adult downies may crush insect prey in their bills before giving it to their young.

Young Downy Woodpeckers solicit food from their parents by begging. When begging, nestling downies utter begging calls and simultaneously extend their heads upward with their mouths wide open. With young nestlings, any change in light intensity in the cavity is enough to stimulate what one observer described as "a frantic, rasping begging response." This response is conducive to efficient feeding, because light levels in a cavity decrease when a parent enters to feed the nestlings. Young downies, however, begin begging even when the reduction in light levels is caused by a cloud or branch or a person's hand casting a shadow over the nest entrance. By the time they are twelve to fifteen days old, nestlings respond less to changes in light intensity and more to the appearance or sounds of their parents.

Although there have been no detailed studies of the begging behavior of young downies, studies of other birds indicate that the nestling that starts to beg first, reaches highest, and holds its beak closest to the parent is most likely to be fed. And for cavity-nesting species like Downy Woodpeckers, reaching highest is undoubtedly the most important factor, because adults deliver food from above. In most bird species, parents do not keep track of which nestlings they feed or make sure that all young receive similar amounts of food; they simply feed the nestling that begs most vigorously. Typically, begging intensity is related to a nestling's hunger level, with intensity increasing as the time since last being fed increases. So the nestlings fed most recently beg less vigorously, and as a result, all nestlings usually receive similar amounts of food from parents.

Nestlings utter lots of begging calls, especially when a parent arrives at the nest cavity. These calls have little to do with determining which nestling will be fed, however. The nestling's position—and more precisely, the position of its open mouth—determines whether it will be fed. If this is so, why utter calls that could attract predators? In one study, adult birds increased their feeding rates when taped begging calls were played over speakers near the nests. Other studies have revealed that calling rates of nestlings increase with hunger level. Thus adult birds can use the collective vocalizing of their nestlings to assess the nestlings' hunger level and adjust their feeding rates. This helps adults bring enough food to ensure that their young continue to grow as they should without bringing more food than is necessary. Bringing too much food would waste parental energy, and the more parental visits to the nest, the greater the chances that a predator will notice the activity and locate the nest.

Nest sanitation is important, because nestling downies produce lots of fecal material, and the parents must remove this material from the nest cavity. Wet, feces-covered nestlings would have trouble keeping warm. An accumulation of fecal material in the nest would provide a perfect environment for bacteria and parasites, which could cause illness or even death. And the odor of accumulating fecal material in the cavity could attract predators. Nest sanitation is made easy for parent birds, because the fecal material of nestlings is enclosed in a tough mucous membrane, forming what is called a fecal sac.

During the first few days after hatching, adult downies eat most of the fecal sacs produced by the nestlings. This helps keep the nest clean, and it also provides the adults with some nutritional benefit, as food passing through the digestive systems of young birds is not completely digested. Fecal sacs produced by older nestlings contain less nutritional value and are normally not consumed by adults. Adults carry fecal sacs in their bills and usually fly some distance from the nest before dropping them.

Male downies are primarily responsible for removal of fecal sacs. Each nestling produces a fecal sac after being fed three or four times, and sacs are usually expelled right after being fed. Adults, especially males, often remain at the nest after feeding a nestling and wait for the fecal sac to be expelled. A nestling often leans forward while an adult, again usually a male, gently pokes the young bird near the cloaca to stimulate ejection of a fecal sac. Males do not remove fecal sacs during each visit.

At hatching, young Downy Woodpeckers weigh about 0.1 to 0.14 ounce (3 to 4 grams). Over the next fourteen to sixteen days, nestlings gain weight at a rate of about 0.05 ounce (1.5 grams) per day. Nestling weight then usually levels off and may actually decline for a few days prior to fledging.

Not all of the food ingested by nestlings goes into growth; some is used for respiration and other body functions, such as producing body heat, and some is used for activity. Throughout the nestling period, about 20 percent of the energy the young gain from parental feeding goes into growth, 60 percent into respiration and maintenance, and 20 percent into activity. Just before fledging, young downies usually weigh about 0.78 to 0.85 ounce (22 to 24 grams), which is about 81 to 89 percent of the typical adult weight of about 0.95 ounce (27 grams).

At hatching, young downies are largely pinkish red and completely naked. Many newly hatched downies show no sign of feathers; others have faint dots on the wings where, in several days, feathers will eventually emerge. The eyes are closed, and will remain so for ten to twelve days. The skin is so thin that digestive organs and blood vessels are clearly visible. The feet and wings are weakly developed. Within a half hour or so after hatching, young downies are able to right themselves, raise their heads, gape, and utter begging notes. Because muscles are still weak, nestlings can only hold their heads up for a second or two on the day of hatching. By the second day, nestlings can hold their heads up for several seconds at a time.

The various body structures of young Downy Woodpeckers do not develop at the same rates. Those structures used most by nestlings develop at the fastest rates. The mouth is of obvious importance to nestling downies, and gape width and bill length increase rapidly during the first several days after hatching. Such changes in mouth size allow older nestlings, with their increasing energy needs, to handle multiple or larger food items. Changes in the shape of the mouth and bill are also important because their functions must change as young downies develop. Initially, the mouth is just a target for adults delivering food, but after fledging, the mouth and bill must become efficient foraging tools.

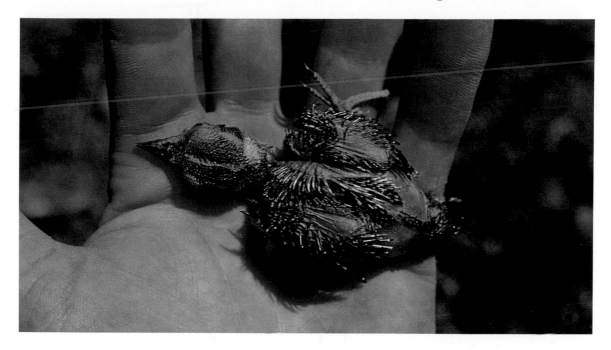

In many species, the mouths of nestlings possess special markings that aid adults in placing food items in the proper position. Nestling downies are no exception. At the base of each side of the lower mandible is a white, knoblike protuberance. These protuberances, which persist until young downies are about eleven or twelve days old, help adult downies accurately deliver food into the mouths of their young, even under the low-light conditions of a cavity.

The legs, including muscles, of nestlings also develop rapidly. This is important because longer, stronger legs improve a nestling's ability to reach higher with greater control, thus enabling it to become better at begging. Development of the leg muscles also improves the ability of nestling downies to produce body heat and maintain body temperature. Birds produce heat by shivering, or the rapid contraction of skeletal muscles, and shivering leg muscles permit nestlings to generate the heat needed to thermoregulate.

The wings of nestling downies develop more slowly than the legs. Though young downies need longer, stronger legs as soon as possible to permit more efficient begging, rapid development of the wings is not as important. Young downies are not capable of even limited flight until about fourteen days old. Their ability to fly then improves, and they are capable of short horizontal flights—maybe 10 to 20 feet—when sixteen days old.

As nestlings develop, their eyes gradually open (about eight to ten days after hatching, shown above), and their plumage begins to develop. Although feathers eventually cover the entire body, they are not initially distributed uniformly. Feathers originate from regions of skin called feather tracts, or pterylae, and these tracts are separated by apteria, areas of skin with few or no feathers. Four to ten days after hatching, feather sheaths emerge from the feather tracts, including those on the wings and tail. Eight to twelve days after hatching, feathers break through the ends of their sheaths. The feathers then grow rapidly and largely cover the apteria by sixteen to eighteen days after hatching. By that time, the primaries range from about one-third to two-thirds the length of adult primaries, and they continue to grow after fledging. The tail feathers, or rectrices, are not quite two-thirds the length of adult tail feathers at fledging.

Nestling downies remain naked longer than nestlings of many other bird species, especially open-cup nesters. However, feathers may be less important for nestling woodpeckers because nest cavities are better insulated and provide more protection from the elements than open nests. In addition, adult downies often brood nestlings for at least a week after hatching, and longer when temperatures are low.

During the first four to seven days after hatching, nestling downies do little except huddle together and raise their heads and gape when an adult arrives with food. Although activity levels increase with increasing age, nestlings at all stages spend most of their time resting— and growing. Very young downies vocalize, producing low-volume *pip-pip-pip* calls plus a longer, rasping note. The *pip* calls are usually given by one or more nestlings between feedings, and the rasping call is uttered by gaping nestlings when adults arrive with food. With increasing age, these calls become louder and lower in frequency.

By four days after hatching, nestling downies are becoming more coordinated and use their legs to begin reaching higher when parents arrive at the nest. By twelve to fourteen days after hatching, shown below and on page 75, young downies can grasp objects firmly with their feet and, if needed, can perch vertically on the inside of the cavity. At this age, nestlings also respond differently to changes in light intensity. Unlike younger downies, nestlings at this age become silent and crouch down when light intensity in the cavity suddenly decreases. If the shadow turns out to be a parent, the nestlings immediately respond with vigorous begging. If not a parent, however, this response by nestlings is beneficial, because a shadow may turn out to be a predator, and quiet, cowering nestlings are less likely to be detected.

When a potential predator approaches a nest occupied by downy nestlings, adults may vigorously defend their young. Louise de Kiriline Lawrence observed a pair of downies defending their nestlings from a red squirrel: "The female woodpecker was inside and she launched a vicious pecking attack at the squirrel. The male on a twig above the nest opening was in full threat appearance, the feathers on head, neck, and shoulders erect, tail spread, and wings wide opened . . . he . . . then flung himself bodily at the enemy, repeating this sequence several times . . . [before] the squirrel gave up and disappeared." Such defense is not unusual, especially as nestlings approach the time of fledging.

9

Fledging and the Postfledging Period

Young Downy Woodpeckers leave the nest, or fledge, about twenty to twenty-five days after hatching. Although typical for cavity nesters, this is a very long nestling period compared with those of birds that nest in the open. Young of open-cup nesters usually fledge ten to twelve days after hatching. This difference in the duration of nestling periods may be due in part to the risk of nest failure. Open-cup nesters suffer higher rates of nest predation, and so it is beneficial for young to leave the nest as soon as possible. Also, the relatively short incubation period of Downy Woodpeckers means that they hatch in a relatively immature condition. As a result, they need more time to grow and develop and therefore require a longer nestling period.

About five to seven days before nest departure, young Downy Woodpeckers first climb to the cavity entrance. Over the next few days, the nestlings spend increasing amounts of time there. Climbing to the entrance during the days prior to fledging is a valuable experience for the nestlings because, to do so, they must firmly grasp the inner walls of the cavity with their feet and move upward, as they'll have to on tree trunks and branches after fledging. This practice no doubt strengthens their leg and tail muscles (strong tail muscles are needed because the tail serves as an important brace for woodpeckers on vertical surfaces).

During this time, young downies are often at the entrance when a parent arrives with food. The presence of a nestling at the entrance may cause adults to alter their approach. Instead of flying directly to the entrance, an adult may land next to or below the hole, move toward the begging nestling, and then extend its bill so that the nestling can reach the food item. An adult flying directly to the entrance would face a bill poking, sometimes inaccurately, at its bill. As the time of fledging approaches, young downies may compete more vigorously with siblings for access to the sometimes less numerous food items.

What induces young Downy Woodpeckers to leave the nest cavity? One important factor is size. Nestlings must achieve a particular level of maturation or development before they can survive outside the nest. A nestling that leaves the nest before it is able to maintain its body temperature or before it has sufficient muscular control to maintain its position on the side of a tree will almost certainly not survive. Once that level of development has been reached, the primary factors involved in determining the time of fledging are probably hunger and sibling competition. In other words, a nestling probably leaves the nest in an attempt to obtain additional feedings from its parents at the expense of its siblings. Once one nestling has left the nest cavity, parents may preferentially feed that nestling. Siblings remaining in the nest, therefore, will not be fed or will be fed less frequently. Hunger will then stimulate them to follow their newly fledged sibling and leave the nest cavity.

Louise de Kiriline Lawrence observed one example in which the eagerness of the young to obtain food led to fledging: "As the parents came with food, the young attacked them. One [nestling] trying eagerly to strip the food from the parent's bill as the adult bird clung to the [entrance], suddenly swung its whole body outside [the cavity]. The deed was done. Once outside, the fledgling hopped aggressively around the trunk in pursuit. When it could not catch up with the father, the fledgling launched itself into flight . . . [and] alighted on a nearby trunk about 25 feet from the nest tree."

In some species, including Downy Woodpeckers, parents may encourage fledging by reducing the number of visits to the nest. Nestlings fed less frequently become hungrier and more aggressive, and they quickly become sufficiently hungry to venture out of the nest in attempt to obtain food from their parents. To once again cite Lawrence: "As the [adult male] came to feed, [nestlings] would pop out . . . with such sudden violence that he had to hop aside to avoid head-on collisions. The impatience of the nestlings increased. In their eagerness to get at the food, they pecked at [the male's] breast and feet, each time just saving themselves from tumbling out." As young downies become increasingly hungry, they may no longer "save themselves" and, instead, leave the cavity in an attempt to obtain food from their parents.

Reduced parental feeding rates near the end of the nestling period may do more than induce fledging of young downies. Less food also means that nestlings may actually lose some weight as the time of fledging approaches. This is likely beneficial, because lighter fledglings probably will be better fliers. Young downies are unable to exercise their flight muscles prior to fledging because of the small size of their nest cavity. Despite this, newly fledged young must be reasonably competent fliers to follow foraging parents and avoid predation. Losing some weight just prior to leaving the nest makes it easier for the unexercised flight muscles and no doubt contributes to the sometimes impressive flying ability of newly fledged downies.

Nestlings often leave the nest cavity late in the morning but may do so at any time of the day. All young in a nest sometimes leave within an hour or less, but departure of the entire brood can take up to twenty-four hours or more. By the time they leave the nest cavity, young males look much like adult males, but lack the red patch at the back of the head. The forehead is black, spotted with white, and there is a red or pink patch on top of the head. The dark areas of the plumage are duller than in adults, and the sides may be finely streaked with black. Young females resemble young males, except that the top of the head is black or black spotted with white.

Because of their long nestling period, newly fledged downies are more advanced in many respects than fledglings of open-cup nesters. Young downies can fly reasonably well at fledging, whereas some young songbirds cannot fly at all for several days after fledging. The plumage of newly fledged downies is also relatively advanced. As Harlo Hadow observed, "Feather development was so complete at fledging that only the remiges, rectrices, and greater remige coverts on the underwing still had sheaths on their bases. Newly fledged birds appeared short-tailed but otherwise completely feathered when seen in the woods."

For as long as nine days after fledging, but usually much less, young downies may remain in the vicinity of the nest cavity, although they do not reenter the cavity. Much of the time, they remain hidden in the foliage of the canopy, camouflaged from potential predators. As young downies become increasingly good fliers, families of Downy Woodpeckers range more widely.

Newly fledged downies are unable to forage for themselves and are dependent on their parents for food. Upon spotting or hearing a nearby adult, fledglings immediately start calling. To alert young to their presence, approaching adults typically utter one or more *pick* calls. The calls given by fledglings are similar to those given during the last few days of the nestling period but are often given at a faster rate and with greater volume. Unlike nestlings, fledglings can and do move about, and these characteristics of their begging calls probably make it easier for parents to locate their fledglings. In addition to vocalizing, fledglings initiate a begging display during which they flick their wings. The intensity of the fledgling's begging increases as an adult gets closer and reaches a peak just prior to being fed. As the adult departs, the fledgling continues to beg, but the intensity of the display gradually diminishes. After being fed several times, and as hunger levels decline, fledglings call and display with reduced vigor. Between feedings, fledglings are usually quiet, although, if they are still hungry, they may continue to utter begging calls, but at lower rates and volume than when adults are nearby.

Recently fledged young respond to an approaching predator or human by becoming motionless and quiet. If captured, young downies immediately begin uttering loud distress calls. Adults respond quickly to the calls of fledglings and approach the potential predator, often vocalizing and flying at the predator. The behavior of the adults may distract the predator and permit the captured fledgling to escape, but more likely, the fledgling will be lost to the predator.

During the days after fledging, young downies become stronger and, as their flight feathers and flight muscles continue to develop, better fliers. By a week after fledging, they can fly very well. They also begin to follow their parents in an attempt to increase the chances of being fed. In contrast to their behavior shortly after fledging, fledglings at this stage are more vocal and much more mobile. Young downies also make their first attempts at foraging for themselves within a few days after fledging. Early attempts to capture prey are usually unsuccessful, but with increasing age and practice, success rates gradually begin to improve. Because of their mobility, fledgling downies at this stage are difficult to observe. Thus, little is known about the process whereby young downies develop their foraging skills. Certain aspects of foraging are no doubt innate, however. For example, the movements involved in using their bills to capture prey probably require little learning. In contrast, when it comes to learning where to forage and precisely what items to select as prey, some learning is likely involved. Some of this learning is probably through trial and error, but fledglings may also acquire important information by following their parents and noting where they forage and what types of food they select.

Two weeks after fledging, young downies are becoming increasingly independent. Fledglings at this age still spend time following and being fed by their parents, but they also move throughout their parents' territory and into adjacent territories on their own. At this stage, the foraging skills of fledglings are continuing to improve, but many, if not most, attempts at capturing insects or other prey are still unsuccessful. Because of their limited foraging success, hungry fledglings are likely to solicit food from their parents. Then, after being fed, they may continue with their own less efficient attempts to find food. Learning to forage efficiently may take several months, and even after becoming independent, young downies are not able to forage as well as adults. Such inefficiency no doubt contributes to the high mortality rates experienced by young Downy Woodpeckers during their first year of life.

Young downies usually become independent of their parents about two and a half to three weeks after leaving the nest. Fledglings may still attempt to obtain food from their parents, but with limited success. Adults may respond aggressively to young that persist in trying to solicit feeding. Lawrence Kilham described one interaction between a female downy and her fledgling: "The mother was going up the trunk of a paper birch . . . when a juvenile flew over, landed, and backed down to within a meter of her. She flew at it, driving it away. But the juvenile was like a leech. Hardly had the mother started to feed again, than the juvenile returned. This time the mother did a bill-waving dance. The juvenile, seemingly undisturbed, stayed where it was. She then drove at it again. The young one was so persistent that it was hard to see how the mother got time to feed. The last I saw of the two was the mother chasing her young one in a fast, circular pursuit through the trees." After a day or two of such treatment, fledglings may cease further attempts at begging and concentrate on their own foraging activity.

After becoming independent, young downies may remain in the vicinity of their parents for several days or even weeks. Some young may even remain in or near parental territories into September or October. All young downies eventually disperse, leaving parental territories and moving to another location, where they eventually breed, if they survive to do so. This movement of young birds is called natal dispersal.

Little is known about the natal dispersal of Downy Woodpeckers. In general, young birds disperse relatively short distances, and most young downies probably move less than a mile from parental territories. Studies of young downies that have been banded to permit the identification of individual birds have revealed that a few juveniles may move much farther, in extreme cases as far as 100 miles or more. In one case, a young female Downy Woodpecker moved 675 miles from her parents' territory.

Dispersing downies face several potential risks. For example, young birds moving through unfamiliar areas may be more vulnerable to predation. But natal dispersal also provides benefits. Moving away from parents and siblings decreases the chances of breeding with near relatives. In addition, young downies may disperse into areas with improved opportunities for obtaining needed resources, such as good foraging sites.

In many species of birds, including Downy Woodpeckers, young females usually disperse farther than young males. The reasons for this sex-biased dispersal are not completely understood. The mating system of downies, and many other birds, may be an important factor. Male downies establish breeding territories that contain resources essential to successful reproduction, and females may choose mates based, at least in part, on differences in the quality of these territories. Young males remaining near their natal territories may be more likely to establish a good-quality territory because familiarity with the area may permit higher feeding rates and lower predation rates. In other words, males remaining as close as possible to their natal territory are more likely to survive and more likely to be in good physical condition. Young females, in contrast, might benefit from sampling a greater number of potential mates and, particularly if inbreeding is detrimental, traveling greater distances as they seek good-quality mates and territories.

Dispersing young may remain in a particular area for just a few hours or days. If, however, a young downy finds an area with abundant food and cavities for roosting, further dispersal may be delayed for many days or even weeks. Before completing dispersal, it is likely that young male downies evaluate areas as potential territories, while young females, particularly as spring approaches, remain on the lookout for potential mates.

After fledging, the main flight feathers (primaries and secondaries) and the tail feathers (rectrices) of young downies continue to grow. Within a week to ten days, these feathers have completed their growth. Even while these flight and tail feathers are growing, young male and female downies begin their first prebasic molt. During this molt, the body plumage, rectrices, and all primary feathers are replaced, but all secondaries and some upper wing coverts are retained. Loss and replacement of the primaries begins with the innermost and proceeds outward. The innermost two primaries of young downies are very short. These abbreviated inner primaries are the first to be lost as the prebasic molt begins, and they typically are replaced even before young downies fledge. These very short feathers require less energy to produce than full-size feathers, so available energy can be diverted to other growing tissues. And because they are replaced before fledging, these small flight feathers cause no disadvantage when young downies must be able to fly.

The first prebasic molt typically ends by September or October. With the completion of this molt, the plumage of young downies, known as the first basic plumage, resembles that of adults. Beginning shortly before fledging, eye color also changes. Nestling or recently fledged downies have a pale gray or olive iris, and this becomes brown or reddish brown during the weeks after fledging.

First-year birds typically suffer high mortality rates, and young downies are no exception. It is likely that 70 to 80 percent of young downies die during their first year of life. Shortly after fledging, high mortality rates are due primarily to predation. Recently fledged downies cannot fly as well as adults and are not as vigilant as adults, so they suffer high rates of predation. Another period of high mortality probably occurs immediately after parents stop feeding fledglings. Studies of other species have revealed that newly independent young birds usually lose weight because they forage less efficiently than adults. Newly independent birds take longer to locate and capture prey items and are more likely than adults to select prey with lower energy content. Not surprisingly, inexperienced juvenile birds typically lose most of their body fat during the first few days of independence. Thereafter, these juveniles must acquire enough food each day to meet their daily energy demands. If not, they will continue to lose weight, and some will die of starvation.

If young downies become sufficiently proficient at foraging to survive the first two or three weeks of independence, their chances of surviving until the next breeding season improve dramatically. Some young downies will be taken by predators, such as Sharp-shinned and Cooper's Hawks, throughout the winter, and some, particularly in harsh winters, may die of starvation, but after the first weeks of juvenile independence, mortality rates for first-year downies probably decline and approach those of adults. Even for adult downies, however, mortality rates are probably about 40 percent. Thus, most downies live for only two to five years, although they may live as long as ten to twelve years.

10

The Nonbreeding Period

After the young disperse, adult Downy Woodpeckers begin to range more widely. Some pairs of downies maintain sufficient contact to prevent complete dissolution of the pair-bond, and these pairs may be among the first to start spending more time together during late winter (January and February) in preparation for the next breeding season.

Once each year, adult Downy Woodpeckers undergo molt, a process by which old feathers are replaced with new ones. This is necessary because over time, feathers begin to show signs of wear and tear. Structurally sound feathers are needed for efficient flight and thermoregulation. In addition, plumage quality and color can be important indicators of sex, age, and condition.

Adult Downy Woodpeckers typically molt during August and September. When molting, all the feathers of a particular area, or feather tract, are not shed simultaneously, and within each feather tract, the sequence of feather loss is consistent from bird to bird. For example, molt of the primaries, or flight feathers, begins with the loss of the innermost feather on each side. As this new feather begins to grow out, the adjacent feather is lost, and so on, until finally the outermost primary is lost. By the time this occurs, replacement of the innermost feathers is nearing completion. Because the molt of flight feathers is gradual and symmetrical, downies are always able to fly.

In most birds, molt of the tail feathers, or rectrices, begins with the loss of the innermost or central pair, then proceeds outward. The outermost tail feathers are lost when the central feathers have been replaced. In downies and most other woodpeckers, however, molt of the tail feathers begins with the second-innermost pair of feathers, and the central pair is replaced last. According to Lester Short, "Since the central pair are the longest and strongest of the rectrices, this means that the central pair are maintained while the other feathers are being lost or regrowing. When the small outermost feathers are shed, and regrowth begins, and after the other lateral feathers have grown to their full size, the central pair are shed. This schedule allows maximum (if somewhat reduced) efficiency of use of the tail in its support or bracing function during the period of molt."

Adult Downy Woodpeckers are usually sedentary. Some investigators have suggested that downies in Canada and the northern United States may occasionally migrate southward during the fall and winter. Recent analysis indicates that downies are permanent residents, however, even at the northern limits of their North American range, and those that do move during the nonbreeding season are dispersing rather than migrating.

Most dispersing downies are juveniles, although some adult downies also disperse. Such movements are termed breeding dispersal. Breeding dispersal is the movement of adults that have reproduced between successive breeding sites, and adult females are more likely to disperse than males. A female downy may disperse if her mate from the previous breeding season dies or is killed by a predator or if she is divorced by or chooses to divorce a previous mate. The term divorce refers to cases where at least one partner re-pairs with another individual while both partners are still alive. Pairs of Downy Woodpeckers sometimes persist for two or more years, but others do not. Divorce may occur when one member of a pair is able to obtain a better-quality mate or when another downy displaces one member of a pair. This could occur if the third downy is dominant over the ousted partner. If a divorce occurs late in the breeding season, the displaced downy may disperse during the nonbreeding season and, while doing so, evaluate other individuals as potential mates. During breeding dispersal, most adult downies travel less than a mile, although movements of 200 miles or more have been reported.

During the nonbreeding period, Downy Woodpeckers often associate with other species of birds. Rarely do these flocks include more than three downies, probably because the presence of more downies would increase competition for foraging sites and food. The other species generally do not compete directly with downies because of differences in foraging behavior and food habits.

Downies in flocks forage more efficiently because they spend less time watching for potential predators. The predators that represent the greatest threat to many other small birds, including downies, are Sharp-shinned and Cooper's Hawks. These fast-flying hawks can pick unwary birds off a branch or tree trunk or, if their prey attempts to elude them, capture it in the air after a rapid, often circuitous, pursuit. Downies watch for these hawks, as well as other potential predators, by turning their heads to the right or left. Such movements, called head-cocks, give downies a much better view of the surrounding area. But downies scanning for predators cannot simultaneously search for food, so more scanning means reduced feeding rates.

Downies in small flocks of two or three birds perform fewer head-cocks per minute than solitary downies, and those in larger flocks, consisting of four or more birds, perform still fewer. Fewer head-cocks translates into more time available for foraging and higher feeding rates.

Downy Woodpeckers in flocks can be less vigilant because the other birds also spend some time watching for predators. Thus, even though each individual may spend less time scanning, collectively the flock spends as much time scanning as a solitary bird, or even more. As a result, assuming that any bird in the flock that spots a predator alerts other flock members, downies are likely to detect approaching predators faster when in flocks than when alone.

Downy Woodpeckers prefer to join flocks with chickadees, titmice, nuthatches, Hairy Woodpeckers, or other downies and only alter their behavior when in a flock with these species. One likely reason for this preference is that chickadees and titmice readily give alarm calls in response to predators, and many other species, including downies, recognize and respond to these calls.

Typically, downies respond by remaining motionless for about ten seconds. In this frozen posture, downies attempt to blend into the tree trunk by pressing their bodies against the trunk, sometimes with the bill pointing straight up. If a downy hears an alarm call while foraging on a small branch, less than about 3 inches in diameter, it flies to a larger branch or tree trunk before freezing. Downies then head-cock at high rates, no doubt in an attempt to determine the location of the apparent predator.

After chickadees or titmice utter an alarm call, all birds in the flock, including downies, stop vocalizing. This silence probably continues as long as flock members perceive a potential threat. Typically, flock members resume normal activities about two to ten minutes after an alarm call. The contact calls of chickadees (*chick-a-dee-dee-dee*) and titmice appear to be the primary "all-clear" signal for birds in mixed-species flocks. Downies pay attention to these signals and resume foraging soon after hearing them. Without benefit of the "all-clear" signals of other species, downies that detect a predator when foraging alone tend to wait longer before resuming foraging. This is another reason that downies in flocks have more time to forage than solitary downies, and during cold winter days, additional time foraging can be very important.

In contrast to chickadees and titmice, Downy Woodpeckers in mixed-species flocks rarely give alarm calls. As part of her Ph.D. research at Rutgers University, Kimberly Sullivan observed the responses of downies to both naturally occurring predators and stuffed predator models and found that downies gave alarm calls only when there was a Downy Woodpecker of the opposite sex (presumably their mate) in the flock. Downies did not give alarm calls when no other downies were present or when just a downy of the same sex was present. These observations indicate that downies give alarm calls only to protect their mates.

Downies probably give few alarm calls because they are more vulnerable to avian predators than chickadees or titmice. Most small birds, like chickadees and titmice, quickly fly into dense cover after giving or hearing alarm calls. Downies, in contrast, are more exposed because their strategy is often to remain motionless on the side of a tree trunk or branch.

To reduce its vulnerability, a Downy Woodpecker will use a branch or trunk as a shield. As a predator moves, the downy also moves in an attempt to keep the branch or trunk between it and the predator. A downy may move completely around the trunk of a tree if a predator circles the tree while trying to get a clear view of its potential meal. Raptor biologist Tom Cade described such behavior during an interaction between a Northern Shrike and a downy. The shrike flew at the woodpecker, "which avoided his attack by dodging around to the other side of the trunk. The shrike then sat on a branch . . . for several seconds before attacking again. The result was always the same: the woodpecker easily avoided him by moving around on the tree trunks."

Although tree trunks and branches may provide protection for downies, they also obstruct the downies' view and can interfere with the detection of predators. As Indiana State University professor Steven Lima points out, this means that downies "must both remain vigilant to predatory attack while feeding, and deal with the visual obstruction provided by its refuge." Downies deal with this problem by occasionally peering around trunks and branches and pulling their heads back to improve their field of view. Downies spend more time doing so when foraging on larger trunks and branches.

During the nonbreeding period, most downies are relatively sedentary. Several factors may contribute to such behavior. First, downies typically spend the winter in or near their breeding territories, and leaving the area, even temporarily, could result in the loss of their territories to an intruding downy. Second, downies often spend the winter near their mates from the previous breeding season, and again, any movement from the area could mean the loss of a mate. And finally, downies roost in cavities during the winter. These cavities protect downies from inclement weather and predators and thus are an important resource. A Downy Woodpecker that strays too far or spends too much time away from its home range risks losing its cavity or cavities to an intruding downy or some other cavity-site competitor.

During the nonbreeding period, as during the breeding season, Downy Woodpeckers spend the night in cavities. Downies typically have more than one roosting cavity because cavities are sometimes lost to competitors, such as squirrels, and trees, snags, and branches containing cavities may be damaged or destroyed during storms. The birds often excavate new cavities during the fall and early winter. The consistency of the wood plus the importance of the cavity (whether the downy has another available or not) determine the time spent excavating a roosting cavity. If no other suitable cavities are available, excavation may take as little as five or six days, and under such circumstances, downies may spend much of the day excavating. More often, however, other cavities are available, and downies spend less time working on the new cavity.

Entrances to Downy Woodpecker roosting cavities may be anywhere from about 5 to 60 feet above ground, with most 7 to 20 feet high. Cavities excavated by females are often lower than those excavated by males, and this difference in preferred heights may help reduce competition among pairs that remain in the same area during the winter. Entrance holes average $1^7/8$ inches in diameter but may range from about $1^1/4$ to $2^3/8$ inches in diameter. The average roosting cavity is 7 inches deep, though they may vary from as shallow as 4 inches to as deep as 10 inches.

Cavity roosts provide concealment and protection from predators. Of equal importance during the winter, cavities represent favorable microclimates that permit downies to save valuable energy. Studies show that roosting cavities excavated by downies during colder weather are deeper, have smaller entrances, and are usually oriented away from prevailing winds. These characteristics reduce heat loss from cavities and, therefore, from downies, and as a result, downies need not expend as much energy to maintain their body temperature. Even small reductions in energy expenditure during cold weather can make the difference between surviving and not surviving.

Conserving energy is very important for Downy Woodpeckers, particularly during cold weather. Downies, like other birds, are endothermic, or warm-blooded, and when active, they maintain a body temperature of about 105 degrees F (41 degrees C). Maintaining this rather high body temperature requires energy, and the amount of energy needed changes with ambient temperature. When the air temperature is above 65 degrees F, downies expend little or no energy to maintain their body temperature. They control body temperature by fluffing up feathers as temperatures decline and changing patterns of blood flow, directing blood away from the body surface so that less heat is lost. When the ambient temperature drops below 65 degrees, however, downies must begin to expend energy to maintain their body temperature.

Throughout much of their range, winter temperatures are usually lower than this—often much lower—and so, for much of the winter, downies must generate more heat and use more energy. As temperatures fall, downies first tense their muscles, especially those of their breast and legs, and then begin to shiver. This muscular activity creates heat but uses a lot of energy. The colder the temperature, the more energy downies must use to stay warm. Finding and then staying in microclimates that provide slightly warmer temperatures and protection from the elements, especially wind, can help downies conserve substantial amounts of energy.

During the night, downies can conserve energy by roosting in cavities. And it is likely that downies conserve additional energy by allowing their body temperature to fall by as much as 10 to 15 degrees F during cold winter nights. This drop in temperature, referred to as nocturnal hypothermia, occurs in several species of birds, including chickadees. Nocturnal hypothermia permits birds to reduce energy expenditure during long winter nights by as much as 10 percent. This savings can be invaluable for downies trying to survive during northern winters when temperatures are low, nights are long, and days—the time available for foraging—are short.

Even during the day, downies can seek out more favorable microclimates. Male downies typically forage higher in the canopy and on smaller branches than females. During colder, windier weather, however, males forage closer to the ground, where wind velocities are reduced, and spend more time on the sides of larger trunks away from the wind. This shift in foraging location—and thus in microclimate—allows males to reduce heat loss and conserve energy. Because female downies normally forage at lower sites, they need not alter their foraging behavior as much as males during inclement weather, but they do shift to somewhat lower sites and spend more time on the leeward side of tree trunks.

During the nonbreeding period, most male and female Downy Woodpeckers occupy ranges of about 10 to 15 acres, although some are as small as 5 acres and others are as large as 30 acres. This is likely due to variation in habitat quality. For example, downies occupying areas with greater numbers of snags would probably have smaller ranges, because snags represent increased food availability and more potential cavity sites. Although they spend most, or perhaps in some cases all, of their time within these ranges, downies will sometimes "commute" long distances ($1/4$ mile or more), and through the ranges of other downies, to visit a particularly good feeding site, such as a feeding station stocked with suet.

Because there is no active defense of boundaries, the winter ranges of individual Downy Woodpeckers overlap considerably. In general, ranges of downies of the opposite sex overlap more than ranges of individuals of the same sex. Because individuals of the same sex tend to forage in the same manner, thus increasing competition for food, and because a downy of the same sex represents a potential competitor for a mate as the breeding season approaches, male and female Downy Woodpeckers are less likely to allow individuals of the same sex to occupy their home ranges.

Although home ranges overlap and are not actively defended, downies seeking access to other needed resources are sometimes involved in aggressive interactions with other individuals. Throughout the winter, such interactions may occur when two or more birds simultaneously try to obtain the same resource. Usually, that resource is food, although downies may also engage in interactions when seeking access to other resources, such as roosting cavities. These resources are typically distributed throughout an area. For example, foraging sites may be distributed relatively evenly throughout a forest or woodlot. In such cases, direct interactions among downies may be uncommon, because individuals usually know their status relative to others and under most circumstances will not directly challenge individuals with higher status than their own. Thus, lower-ranked downies will usually not attempt to drive away a higher-ranked downy, and lower-ranked individuals will usually move away at the approach of a higher-ranked individual.

Several factors may contribute to determining a downy's status or rank relative to others. Two important factors are sex and age. Male downies are usually dominant to females, and older downies are usually dominant to first-year birds. Within sex and age classes, the factors that influence status are not always apparent. One factor that may influence the outcome of such interactions is the location of the interaction. Status among birds, probably including Downy Woodpeckers, is often site-dependent, with individuals more likely to win encounters when in or near their former breeding ranges. So, for example, a male competing with another male for a good foraging site is more likely to win if the encounter takes place in an area that was part of his previous year's breeding territory. If the same two males encounter each other in another location, the outcome may be different.

When needed resources are clumped, interactions between Downy Woodpeckers may be more frequent. This is what occurs at bird feeders. Here, food is abundant and, unlike in more natural environments, found at just one location. Many downies may be attracted to this single location. Even at feeders, however, downies engage in few encounters, and those that occur are usually limited to a quick display. Rarely do downies fight. This is because they recognize their status or rank relative to others, and to avoid wasting energy and possible injury, lower-ranked individuals defer to higher-ranked ones. When fights occur, it is probably because two individuals have similar status and it is not clear which should defer to the other. Such fights are normally brief, with the individuals involved quickly determining their relative status.

Other species are attracted to feeding stations as well. Interspecific fights are also uncommon, with dominance among species, and thus access to resources, generally determined by body size. Larger birds, such as Hairy Woodpeckers, are dominant to smaller ones, such as Downy Woodpeckers. As a result, downies seeking to eat must wait until hairies have finished feeding or attempt to obtain food in a furtive manner while a hairy is feeding.

About 60 percent of adult downies survive from one year to the next. Mortality rates for younger downies are even higher. Some mortality occurs during the breeding season, but most occurs during the nonbreeding period. Death sometimes results from diseases or parasites. For example, feather parasites may reduce the insulating capacity of plumage, and the resulting loss of body heat may increase mortality during cold weather.

Poor nutrition also could affect winter survival, particularly for females. How can you determine a bird's nutritional condition? Tom Grubb, a professor at Ohio State University, found that the speed at which new feathers grow is influenced by a bird's nutritional condition. So, to determine a bird's condition, an investigator can capture the bird, pluck one of its tail feathers, then recapture it at least a month later to determine how rapidly the replacement (or induced) feather grew. This can be determined because the new feathers develop a "growth bar" every twenty-four hours. These growth bars are alternating dark and light bands, with the dark bands produced during the day and the light ones at night. It is not clear why these bands develop, but one dark band plus one light band represent twenty-four hours of feather growth, and the wider the growth bars, the better a bird's nutritional condition.

A study of Downy Woodpeckers conducted during mid-winter (January and February) in Ohio revealed that growth rates of induced feathers were faster for females located in woodlots where supplemental food (feeding stations with sunflower seeds and suet) was available than for females in "unsupplemented" woodlots. No such difference in growth rates was noted for male downies. These results suggest three things. First, at least some female Downy Woodpeckers may be nutritionally stressed (that is, not getting as much food as needed) during the winter, particularly at more northerly locations. Second, male downies may be in better condition during the winter than females. This is likely true because males tend to be dominant over females and, as a result, exclude females from good foraging sites. Finally, nutritionally stressed females may suffer higher mortality rates during the winter.

Death may not result directly from starvation, but downies in poor condition are more likely to die in other ways. For example, weakened downies would be less able to elude pursuing predators. High on the list of predators that might prey on downies during the non-breeding period are Sharp-shinned Hawks, shown here, and Cooper's Hawks. During the winter, many of these hawks move south from their breeding grounds and prey on downies and other birds.

11

Relations with Humans

Prior to the arrival of Europeans in the eastern United States, there were vast areas of old-growth forest. Early writings suggest that the eastern forests were not composed entirely of large, old trees, however. Rather, these forests had many openings and many areas at earlier stages of succession. This complex landscape was produced in part by natural forces such as fires caused by lightning. However, the most important factor was likely the fires set by Native Americans. The regular burning of forests produced several important benefits, including the creation of better habitat for game species, improved visibility (which may have improved hunting success), easier travel through the forest, and the release of nutrients that fertilized the soil (for corn crops). This heterogeneous forest provided plenty of excellent habitat for Downy Woodpeckers.

With the arrival of European settlers, the eastern forests were cut at ever-increasing rates. As this deforestation began, many small openings were produced and much edge habitat was created. Because downies do quite well in such habitat, these early changes probably had little effect on them and may, in fact, have been beneficial. As deforestation continued, however, Downy Woodpecker populations no doubt declined. During the 1700s and 1800s, large areas were deforested, and downy populations in those areas declined dramatically.

From the late 1800s and into the present, reforestation of many areas, particularly in the northeastern United States, began as marginal agricultural areas were abandoned. These second-growth forests have created good habitat for downies and many other woodland species, although downies likely are still less abundant than during presettlement times.

Only since 1966, with the beginning of the Breeding Bird Survey, has there been a systematic means of monitoring bird populations in North America. Each year, participants survey thirty-seven hundred routes throughout the United States and southern Canada. Analysis of data gathered since 1966 indicates that Downy Woodpecker populations in the United States and Canada have remained stable. In contrast, the populations of many other birds, particularly some grassland species and a variety of Neotropical migrant songbirds, have declined. Downy Woodpeckers have two advantages over many other birds. First, because they are not migratory, downies are not affected by habitat destruction in Mexico and Central and South America. And secondly, downies have rather broad habitat requirements. Thus they are less affected by urbanization and other habitat alteration than many other species.

Although downy populations have remained stable on a continent-wide scale for the past three decades, populations in particular areas fluctuate. Downies require trees, and they will not be found in areas where trees are removed. Thus, no downies will be found where large expanses of land have been cleared for agriculture, mining, or other reasons. And not all areas with trees will necessarily support populations of downies. Habitats have become highly fragmented in many parts of North America, with woodlots of various sizes isolated from other wooded areas by cropland, pastures, and new subdivisions. Studies suggest that such isolated woodlots must be at least 2 or 3 acres in size to support a pair of Downy Woodpeckers. Woodlots smaller than this simply do not contain sufficient resources, such as foraging sites and snags, to support downies over an extended period of time.

Because overall populations are stable, any losses of Downy Woodpecker habitat are being balanced by gains in available habitat. This new habitat develops as logged areas undergo succession and, over several years, former open areas become young woods and forests suitable for use by downies. A similar process takes place in urban areas.

Downy Woodpeckers can be found in many urban areas. Most such areas do not provide optimal habitat, however, and as a result, the number of downies present is typically lower than in nearby forested areas. In general, insect-eating birds that forage on bark, like most woodpeckers, or in the canopy of trees are not as common in urban areas because there are fewer trees and therefore fewer foraging sites. In more natural habitats, downies also forage on small trees and shrubs in the understory, but there is typically less understory vegetation in urban areas. Also absent or nearly absent from most urban areas are snags. To most people, dead trees and dead branches represent eyesores and potential hazards, and as a result, these are usually quickly removed. Without these important foraging sites and potential cavity sites, downies are less likely to remain in an area. Because good-quality cavity sites are essential for successful reproduction, downies may avoid urban areas that lack snags or other potential cavity sites during the breeding season.

Also contributing to the reduced numbers of downies in urban areas is the often extensive use of non-native trees and shrubs. Studies have revealed that non-native vegetation often supports fewer species of insects than native trees, and this means less food available for insectivorous species like Downy Woodpeckers.

From the human point of view, Downy Woodpeckers and other insectivorous birds play several valuable roles in forest habitats. Woodpeckers, including downies, are the most important predators of a variety of bark beetles and wood-boring insects. Downies and other insectivorous birds play essential roles in limiting insect populations and, therefore, insect damage to trees.

Beyond simply eating insect pests, downies and other woodpeckers alter the microhabitats where insects are found and, in so doing, reduce the chances that those insects will survive. Woodpeckers puncture or drill into bark and remove, or flake off, pieces of bark. Attached to these small pieces of bark may be insect eggs or larvae that are unlikely to survive a winter on the ground. The foraging activity of downies and other woodpeckers also tends to reduce the overall thickness of tree bark. This thinner bark offers less protection from the elements, particularly cold temperatures, and as a result, insect pests attempting to overwinter in the bark may suffer higher rates of mortality.

Many woodpeckers, including downies, sometimes select man-made objects, such as metal gutters, drainpipes, chimney caps, plumbing vents, and television antennas as drumming sites. These are superb drumming sites, because their resonant qualities permit the production of relatively high-volume, and therefore long-distance, signals. Such drumming occurs most often during late winter and early spring, when woodpeckers are initiating their breeding activities. The extent to which individual woodpeckers drum on these objects varies from once or twice on a single day to persistent use over several weeks or even months.

Downy Woodpeckers engaged in such activity are unlikely to produce substantial damage because of their relatively small size and bills; however, they can produce a great deal of noise. More damage is possible when, as occasionally happens, a woodpecker selects a house as a foraging site.

Woodpeckers that have selected man-made objects as drumming or foraging sites can be very persistent and difficult to deter. As recommended by the U.S. Fish and Wildlife Service, the first step in eliminating the problem is to check the site or sites of woodpecker activity for signs of insect infestation. If insects, such as carpenter ants, carpenter bees, or cluster flies, are found, consult with a licensed pest control operator to determine how to eliminate the insects and prevent future problems. If there are no signs of insects, the only alternative is to try to frighten the birds away by placing such objects as balloons, wind chimes, a child's pinwheel, strings of tin can lids, or strips of aluminum foil at the site of woodpecker activity. If drumming is the problem, cover or wrap the drumming site with padding or provide an alternate drumming site away from the house. A simple "drum" can be made by firmly securing a board to a tree (keeping in mind that woodpeckers prefer relatively high drumming sites) and placing another board over it. The overlapping board should be nailed to the first one only at the top end. Although not essential, covering the overlapping board with metal sheeting may make the drum even more attractive to woodpeckers.

Many people throughout the United States and Canada assist Downy Woodpeckers and other birds by providing food at feeding stations. Studies indicate that supplemental feeding, in the form of sunflower seeds and suet, can improve the nutritional condition of downies, particularly females, and such improvements can, in turn, result in increased survivorship. Downies that visit feeding stations may be in better condition and more likely to survive the winter. As a result, Downy Woodpecker populations may be higher in areas where feeders are present, and feeding may have a direct effect on Downy Woodpecker populations in many areas of North America because increasing numbers of people are putting out food.

Attracting Downy Woodpeckers is relatively easy. A feeding station containing sunflower seeds and suet should, after allowing some time for birds to find the new food source, bring in any nearby downies. Although they readily consume sunflower seeds, suet is even more appealing to downies because of its high energy content. Downies are especially fond of suet during the winter, because the energy it represents can be particularly valuable when temperatures and food availability are low. Downies will, however, feed on suet throughout the year. At temperatures below about 70 degrees F (21 degrees C), suet is solid and it's safe to simply provide the raw fat for downies. At higher temperatures, suet begins to melt or turn rancid. Downies that regularly feed on melted or rancid suet are likely to get some on their feathers, especially at the base of the bill and, to a lesser degree, the rest of the head. As a result, feather follicles around the bill may become inflamed and the feathers lost. This potential problem can be avoided by providing rendered suet, which has a higher melting point, during warmer weather. Commercially available suet cakes are made of rendered suet, and it's also possible to make your own.

To render suet, according to Terry Ross of the Baltimore Bird Club, it's best to start with beef fat that is either ground or chopped into very small pieces. Heat the suet over medium heat until all the fat leaches out. There should be nothing pink in your pan, only solid gray bits in a clear liquid. Strain out the solids by pouring the melted suet through fine cheesecloth. Save the strained liquid fat and let it cool. Suet at this stage is still soft, but repeating the process of melting and straining will produce a very hard suet. This rendered suet can be used as is, made into suet cakes, or stored in the freezer for later use.

Most commercially available suet cakes are mixtures of rendered suet plus such things as millet, sunflower seeds, peanuts or peanut butter, and raisins. Such mixes will attract a greater variety of birds—both suet and seed-eating species—but downies will concentrate on the suet and largely ignore the other items. Seed-eating birds, in contrast, will concentrate on the seeds and ignore the suet. As a result, both suet and seeds may be wasted. It may be better to offer suet and seeds separately to reduce waste and to reduce competition for access to food.

Suet can be provided to downies in several ways. Raw suet can be offered in mesh bags, such as onion or potato bags; small wire cages, which are commercially available; or custom-made cages made of hardware cloth. These suet feeders can be hung or attached to tree trunks, branches, or bird feeders.

Suet can also be warmed and softened, then smeared onto the bark of a tree or pressed into the crevices of large pine cones or into 1-inch-diameter holes drilled into a 2- to 4-inch-diameter section of tree limb perhaps 1 to 3 feet long. Pine cones and suet-filled limbs can then be hung from branches or other structures.

Downies and many other birds, like chickadees, titmice, and nuthatches, have no problem feeding on suet on hanging feeders, and hanging feeders are probably less likely to be raided by opossums, raccoons, and other animals than those that are firmly attached to a trunk or branch. Starlings also like suet, and these aggressive birds may deter other species, including downies, from visiting suet feeders. To discourage starlings, place suet in a cage covered on all sides but the bottom. Birds that will eat suet while hanging upside down, like downies, chickadees, titmice, and nuthatches, will still come to this type of feeder, but birds that have difficulty doing so, like starlings, will probably not.

Downies also like sunflower seeds, and most types of feeders will attract downies, including platform feeders and hanging feeders. Sunflower seeds are rich in fat and protein, and as a result, they are readily eaten by many species of birds. Downies will eat either striped or black oil sunflower seeds, but black oil seeds may be preferred because of their smaller size, which makes them easier to manipulate, and relatively high oil content.

Downies are most easily attracted to feeding stations, and attracted in greater numbers, during the winter, though they will often continue to visit throughout the year. Once the breeding season begins, it is likely that fewer downies will visit a feeder, because the feeder may become part of one pair's breeding range and, particularly if the feeder is near the nesting cavity, that pair may keep other downies away. Food availability also increases with warmer weather, and as a result, downies may visit feeders less frequently, and those located farther away are less likely to make the trip to a feeding station.

A well-stocked feeding station will attract downies and permit brief glimpses of some of the behaviors described in this book. Providing downies with other important requirements, such as foraging sites, potential nesting and roosting sites, and water will allow for more detailed, and varied, observations.

During prolonged dry periods and extended periods of subfreezing temperatures, water can become a scarce resource. Downies get some water from their food, particularly during warmer weather, when more insects are available, but they always require access to water. Water can be provided in a number of ways, ranging from an upside-down garbage can lid to an in-ground pool or pond to a birdbath. Most important, make sure that the water container provides a gradual incline into the water and that it is always filled with water. During northern winters, water can be kept ice-free by using commercially available water heaters.

Trees and shrubs that provide foraging sites will also attract downies. Appropriate species vary with geographic location. For example, downies in Illinois often forage on white oaks and snags; those in New York on elms, white oaks, aspen, and staghorn sumac; and those in Pennsylvania on tulip trees, oaks, and box elder. Even if such trees are present, keep in mind that individual downies will forage at a variety of sites over areas ranging from 5 to 30 acres and therefore will only spend a limited amount of time in a specific area like your backyard.

Downies will spend more time where you can observe them if roosting or nesting sites are available. The best, and often only, way to attract roosting or nesting downies is to provide snags. One way to create snags is to girdle trees. This would be frowned upon in most urban areas, but where possible, it can help increase populations of cavity-nesting birds like Downy Woodpeckers. Ideally, trees to be girdled should not be important wildlife-attracting trees (such as oaks) and should be at least 8 to 12 inches in diameter. To girdle a tree, use an ax to remove a 3- to 4-inch band of bark around the entire circumference of the tree. The cut should go at least an inch below the bark. Girdling kills the tree because the flow of food and water between the roots and the rest of the tree is disrupted. Such trees will soon provide downies and many other organisms with foraging sites and potential cavity sites.

If you would like to attract downies but would rather not girdle trees, an alternative is to find snags elsewhere and place them where desired. Ideally, locate downed logs or branches about 7 or 8 inches in diameter and 8 or more feet long that are slightly but not too decayed. These snags can then be wired in a vertical position to fence posts or, by using a post-hole digger or shovel to dig a suitable support hole, placed anywhere downies are likely to find them. Downies are most likely to excavate cavities in such snags during the fall (for roosting) and during late winter or early spring (for nesting).

Yet another way to attract roosting or nesting downies is to provide artificial snags. Several investigators have found that downies will excavate roosting cavities in polystyrene (bead board) cylinders. The cylinders used in these studies were about 9 inches in diameter and 8 feet long and painted with brown latex enamel to mimic tree color. To support these artificial snags, drill a $1^1/_4$-inch hole about 30 inches longitudinally into one end. Then slide the cylinder down over a metal post driven into the ground.

Studies in Ohio and Texas revealed that downies will excavate roosting cavities in these bead board snags. Fifty of these snags were placed in a woodlot in the Ohio study, and downies excavated cavities in forty-two of them. Twenty-three of forty-seven cylinders were used by downies in the Texas study. Although used by many roosting downies, the cavities excavated in these artificial snags were never used by nesting downies. It is likely that polystyrene is simply too soft—like well-decayed wood—to suit nesting downies. Nest cavities in soft substrates are more likely to be predated because they can be easily opened by predators like raccoons. Although nesting downies did not use the cavities excavated in the polystyrene snags, they were subsequently used by a variety of secondary cavity nesters, including chickadees, house wrens, and flying squirrels.

Efforts to attract downies will be amply rewarded with additional opportunities to observe our smallest woodpecker and other birds using the resources provided. As stated by Fannie Eckstorm in 1901: "Most birds do not stay all the year . . . and most demand some portion of the fruit or grain of midsummer and autumn. Not so Downy. His services are entirely gratuitous; he works twice as long as most others. He spends the year with us, no winter ever too severe for him, no summer too hot. If in the cold winter weather we will take pains to hang out . . . a piece of suet . . . we may see how he appreciates our thoughtfulness. If his cousin the hairy and his neighbor the chickadee come and eat with him, bid them a hearty welcome. The feast is spread for all the birds that help men, and friend Downy shall be their host."

References

Adkisson, C. S. 1988. Cavity-nesting birds of North America: past history, present status, and future prospects, pp. 85–100. In *Bird conservation* 3 (J. A. Jackson, ed.). Univ. Wisconsin Press, Madison.

Anderson, S. H., and H. H. Shugart, Jr. 1974. Habitat selection of breeding birds in an east Tennessee deciduous forest. *Ecology* 55:828–37.

Ball, R. M., Jr., and J. C. Avise. 1992. Mitochondrial DNA phylogeographic differentiation among avian populations and the evolutionary significance of subspecies. *Auk* 109:626–36.

Beal, F. E. L. 1911. Food of the woodpeckers of the United States. U.S. Dept. Agric., *Biol. Surv. Bull.* No. 37.

Beissinger, S. R., and D. R. Osborne. 1982. Effects of urbanization on avian community organization. *Condor* 84:75–83.

Bent, A. C. 1939. Life histories of North American woodpeckers. Smithsonian Inst. *U.S. Natl. Mus. Bull.* 174. Washington, D.C.

Bock, W. J. 1964. Kinetics of the avian skull. *J. Morph.* 114:1–42.

Browning, M. R. 1995. Do Downy Woodpeckers migrate? *J. Field Ornithol.* 66:12–21.

Burchsted, A. E. 1987. Downy Woodpecker caches food. *Wilson Bull.* 99:136–37.

Cade, T. J. 1962. Wing movements, hunting, and displays of the Northern Shrike. *Wilson Bull.* 74:386–408.

Clark, G. A., Jr. 1969. Oral flanges of juvenile birds. *Wilson Bull.* 81:270–79.

Conner, R. N. 1980. Foraging habits of woodpeckers in southwestern Virginia. *J. Field Ornithol.* 51:119–27.

——1981. Seasonal changes in woodpecker foraging patterns. *Auk* 98:562–70.

Conner, R. N., and C. S. Adkisson. 1976. Discriminant function analysis: a possible aid in determining the impact of forest management on woodpecker nesting habitat. *Forest Sci.* 22:122–27.

——1977. Principal component analysis of woodpecker nesting habitat. *Wilson Bull.* 89:122–29.

Conner, R. N., and D. Saenz. 1996. Woodpecker excavation and use of cavities in polystyrene snags. *Wilson Bull.* 108:449–56.

Crusoe, D. A. 1980. Acoustic behavior and its role in the social relations of the Red-headed Woodpecker. M.S. thesis, Univ. Illinois–Chicago Circle.

Dodenhoff, D. J. 1996. Interspecific and intraspecific communication: a quantitative analysis of drumming behavior using four species of California-occurring woodpeckers (Family Picidae). M.S. thesis, California Polytechnic St. Univ., San Luis Obispo.

Duncan, S. D. 1990. Auditory communication in breeding Northern Flickers. Ph.D. diss., Univ. Wisconsin–Milwaukee.

Eckstorm, F. H. 1901. The woodpeckers. Houghton Mifflin and Co., New York.

George, W. G. 1972. Age determination of Hairy and Downy Woodpeckers in eastern North America. *Bird-Banding* 43:128–35.

Gordon, A. L., and J. L. Confer. 1996. Do Downy Woodpeckers abandon their breeding territories in winter and relocate near a permanent food source? *Kingbird* 46:111–16.

Grubb, T. C., Jr. 1975. Weather-dependent foraging behavior of some birds wintering in a deciduous woodland. *Condor* 77:175–82.

——·1982. Downy Woodpecker sexes select different cavity sites: an experiment using artificial snags. *Wilson Bull.* 94:577–79.

——·1989. Ptilochronology: feather growth bars as indicators of nutritional status. *Auk* 106:314–20.

Grubb, T. C., Jr., and D. A. Cimprich. 1990. Supplementary food improves the nutritional condition of wintering woodland birds: evidence from ptilochronology. *Ornis Scand.* 21:277–81.

Grubb, T. C., Jr., and M. S. Woodrey. 1990. Sex, age, intraspecific dominance status, and the use of food by birds wintering in temperate-deciduous and cold-coniferous woodlands: a review. *Stud. Avian Biol.* 13:270–79.

Hadow, H. H. 1976. Growth and development of nestling Downy Woodpeckers. *North Amer. Bird Bander* 1:155–64.

Hansen, A. J., and S. Rohwer. 1986. Coverable badges and resource defense in birds. *Anim. Behav.* 34:69–76.

Hawkins, J. A., and G. Ritchison. 1996. Provisioning of nestlings by male and female Downy Woodpeckers. *Kentucky Warbler* 72:79–81.

Jackson, J. A. 1971. The adaptive significance of reversed sexual dimorphism in tail length of woodpeckers: an alternative hypothesis. *Bird-Banding* 42:18–20.

——·1976. How to determine the status of a woodpecker nest. *Living Bird* 15:205–21.

Jackson, J. A., and E. E. Hoover. 1975. A potentially harmful effect of suet on woodpeckers. *Bird-Banding* 46:131–34.

James, F. C. 1970. Geographic size variation in birds and its relationship to climate. *Ecology* 51:365–90.

Johnson, L. S., and L. H. Kermott. 1994. Nesting success of cavity-nesting birds using natural tree cavities. *J. Field Ornithol.* 65:36–51.

Kaufman, K. 1993. Identifying the Hairy Woodpecker. *Amer. Birds* 47:311–14.

Kilham, L. 1962. Reproductive behavior of Downy Woodpeckers. *Condor* 64:126–33.

——·1974. Copulatory behavior of Downy Woodpeckers. *Wilson Bull.* 86:23–34.

——·1974. Early breeding season behavior of Downy Woodpeckers. *Wilson Bull.* 86:407–18.

——·1983. *Life history studies of woodpeckers of eastern North America*. Nuttall Ornithol. Club, Cambridge, MA.

Koplin, J. R. 1969. The numerical response of woodpeckers to insect prey in a subalpine forest in Colorado. *Condor* 71:436–38.

Kroll, J. C., and R. R. Fleet. 1979. Impact of woodpecker predation on over-wintering within-tree populations of the southern pine beetle, pp. 269-81. In *The role of insectivorous birds in forest ecosystems* (J. G. Dickson, R. N. Conner, R. R. Fleet, J. C. Kroll, and J. A. Jackson, eds.). Academic Press, New York.

Li, P., and T. E. Martin. 1991. Nest-site selection and nesting success of cavity-nesting birds in high elevation forest drainages. *Auk* 108:405–18.

Liknes, E. T., and D. L. Swanson. 1996. Seasonal variation in cold tolerance, basal metabolic rate, and maximal capacity for thermogenesis in White-breasted Nuthatches *Sitta carolinensis* and Downy Woodpeckers *Picoides pubescens*, two unrelated arboreal temperate residents. *J. Avian Biol.* 27:279–88.

Lima, S. L. 1992. Vigilance and foraging substrate: anti-predatory considerations in a non-standard environment. *Behav. Ecol. Sociobiol.* 30:283–89.

Mahan, T. A. 1996. Analysis of the acoustic signals of adult male and female Downy Woodpeckers. M.S. thesis, Eastern Kentucky Univ., Richmond.

Marsh, R. E. 1983. Woodpeckers, pp. E79–E84. In *Prevention and control of wildlife damage* (R. M. Timm, ed.). Univ. Nebraska, Lincoln.

Martin, T. E. 1993. Evolutionary determinants of clutch size in cavity-nesting birds: nest predation or limited breeding opportunities? *Am. Nat.* 142:937–46.

Martin, T. E., and P. Li. 1992. Life history traits of open- vs. cavity-nesting birds. *Ecology* 73:579–92.

Matthysen, E., D. Cimprich, and T. C. Grubb, Jr. 1993. Home ranges and social behaviour of the Downy Woodpecker *Picoides pubescens* in winter. *Belg. J. Zool.* 123:193–201.

Matthysen, E., T. C. Grubb, Jr., and D. Cimprich. 1991. Social control of sex-specific foraging behaviour in Downy Woodpeckers. *Anim. Behav.* 42:515–17.

Meyer, W., T. Bartels, K. Neurand, and N. Lange. 1993. Specific structural features of the woodpecker bill, as revealed by direct magnifying microfocal radiography. *Eur. Arch. Biol.* 104:149–55.

Moulton, C. A., and L. W. Adams. 1991. Effects of urbanization on foraging strategy of woodpeckers, pp. 67–73. In *Wildlife conservation in metropolitan environments* (L. W. Adams and D. L. Leedy, eds.). Nat. Inst. Urban Wildl., Columbia, MD.

Norberg, R. A. 1981. Why foraging birds in trees should climb and hop upwards rather than downwards. *Ibis* 123:281–88.

Otvos, I. S. 1979. The effects of insectivorous bird activities in forest ecosystems: an evaluation, pp. 341–74. In *The role of insectivorous birds in forest ecosystems* (J. G. Dickson, R. N. Connor, R. R. Fleet, J. A. Jackson, and J. C. Kroll, eds.). Academic Press, New York.

Otvos, I. S., and R. W. Stark. 1985. Arthropod food of some forest-inhabiting birds. *Can. Entomol.* 117:971–90.

Peterson, A. W., and T. C. Grubb, Jr. 1983. Artificial trees as a cavity substrate for woodpeckers. *J. Wildl. Manage.* 47:790–98.

Petit, D. R., K. E. Petit, T. C. Grubb, Jr., and L. J. Reichhardt. 1985. Habitat and snag selection by woodpeckers in a clear-cut: an analysis using artificial snags. *Wilson Bull.* 97:525–33.

Pyle, P., and S. N. G. Howell. 1995. Flight-feather molt patterns and age in North American woodpeckers. *J. Field Ornithol.* 66:564–81.

Ritchison, G. 1997. The effects of transmitter weight on the behavior and movements of Downy Woodpeckers. *Kentucky Warbler* 73:40–44.

Schroeder, R. L. 1982. *Habitat suitability index models: Downy Woodpecker*. U.S. Dept. Int., Fish Wildl. Serv., FWS/OBS-82/10.38.

Seveyka, J. 1996. Pecking in an arc or a line: what kinematic strategies do woodpeckers employ during excavation? Poster presentation, Annual Meeting of the Society of Integrative and Comparative Biology. *Amer. Zool.* 36(5):133A.

Short, L. L. 1971. Systematics and behavior of some North American woodpeckers, genus *Picoides* (Aves). *Bull. Amer. Mus. Nat. Hist.* 145:1–118.

——·1979. Burdens of the picid hole-excavating habit. *Wilson Bull.* 91:16–28.

——·1982. *Woodpeckers of the world.* Delaware Mus. Nat. Hist., Greenville.

Sibley, C. G. 1957. The abbreviated inner primaries of nestling woodpeckers. *Auk* 74:102–3.

Spring, L. W. 1965. Climbing and pecking adaptations in some North American woodpeckers. *Condor* 67:457–88.

Staebler, A. E. 1949. A comparative life history study of the Downy and Hairy Woodpeckers. Ph.D. diss., Univ. Michigan, Ann Arbor.

Stark, R. D., D. J. Dodenhoff, and E. V. Johnson. 1998. A quantitative analysis of woodpecker drumming. *Condor* 100:350–56.

Sullivan, K. A. 1984. The advantages of social foraging in Downy Woodpeckers *Picoides pubescens*. Ph.D. diss., Rutgers Univ., Newark, NJ.

——·1984. Information exploitation by Downy Woodpeckers in mixed-species flocks. *Behaviour* 91:294–311.

——·1985. Selective alarm calling by Downy Woodpeckers in mixed-species flocks. *Auk* 102:184–87.

——·1985. Vigilance patterns in Downy Woodpeckers. *Anim. Behav.* 33:328–29.

Swierczewski, E. V., and R. J. Raikow. 1981. Hindlimb morphology, phylogeny and classification of the Piciforms. *Auk* 98:466–80.

Tobalske, B. W. 1996. Scaling of muscle composition, wing morphology, and intermittent flight behavior in woodpeckers. *Auk* 113:151–77.

Travis, J. 1977. Seasonal foraging in a Downy Woodpecker population. *Condor* 79:371–75.

Troll, R. 1990. Location of tunnels on goldenrod ball galls made by Downy Woodpeckers. *Trans. Illinois State Acad. Sci.* 83:195–96.

Volman, S. F., T. C. Grubb, Jr., and K. C. Schuett. 1997. Relative hippocampal volume in relation to food-storing behavior in four species of woodpeckers. *Brain Behav. Evol.* 49:110–20.

Williams, J. B. 1975. Habitat utilization by four species of woodpeckers in a central Illinois woodland. *Amer. Midl. Nat.* 93:354–67.

——·1980. Intersexual niche partitioning in Downy Woodpeckers. *Wilson Bull.* 92:439–51.

Williams, J. B., and G. O. Batzli. 1979. Winter diet of a bark-foraging guild of birds. *Wilson Bull.* 91:126–31.

——·1979. Interference competition and niche shifts in the bark-foraging guild in central Illinois. *Wilson Bull.* 91:400–411.

Wilson, A. 1832. *American ornithology*, vol. 1. Chatto and Windus, London.

Wilson, W. H., Jr. 1994. The distribution of wintering birds in central Maine: the interactive effects of landscape and bird feeders. *J. Field Ornithol.* 65:512–19.

Winkler, H., D. A. Christie, and D. Nurney. 1995. *Woodpeckers: a guide to the woodpeckers of the world.* Houghton Mifflin Co., New York.

Winkler, H., and L. L. Short. 1978. A comparative analysis of acoustical signals in pied woodpeckers (Aves, *Picoides*). *Bull. Amer. Mus. Nat. Hist.* 160:1–109.

Yom-Tov, Y., and A. Ar. 1993. Incubation and fledging durations of woodpeckers. *Condor* 95:282–87.

Photo Credits

About the Author

Gary Ritchison is a professor of Biological Sciences at Eastern Kentucky University. He has published in numerous ornithological journals, has presented papers to several academic societies on the behavior and ecology of a variety of bird species, and is the author of Stackpole's *Wild Bird Guides: Northern Cardinal*. He lives in Richmond, Kentucky.

Index